HOW TO BECOME A **MAIN STREET MILLIONAIRE**
HELPING OTHERS GET WHAT THEY NEED

UNCONVENTIONAL
WEALTH

Published by CelebrityPress®, Orlando, FL

CelebrityPress® is a registered trademark.

Printed in the United States of America.

ISBN: 978-0-9907064-0-3
LCCN: 2014948325

This publication is designed to provide accurate and authoritative information with regard to the subject matter covered. It is sold with the understanding that the publisher is not engaged in rendering legal, accounting, or other professional advice. If legal advice or other expert assistance is required, the services of a competent professional should be sought. The opinions expressed by the authors in this book are not endorsed by Celebrity Press®, Steve Forbes, or Forbes Magazine, and are the sole responsibility of the author rendering the opinion.

Most CelebrityPress® titles are available at special quantity discounts for bulk purchases for sales promotions, premiums, fundraising, and educational use. Special versions or book excerpts can also be created to fit specific needs.

For more information, please write:
CelebrityPress®
520 N. Orlando Ave, #2
Winter Park, FL 32789
or call 1.877.261.4930

Visit us online at: www.CelebrityPressPublishing.com

HOW TO BECOME A **MAIN STREET MILLIONAIRE**
HELPING OTHERS GET WHAT THEY NEED

UNCONVENTIONAL WEALTH

By
Mike Conlon
aka
The Main $treet Millionaire

I need to thank a lot of people for helping me with my book. My wife Becky and my kids, Alyssa, Michael, Nick, Maiya, and Marcus for being so supportive and giving me the time to get this book written. Also to my home office team and all our managers at ACG, especially my Chief Operations Officer Chris Barry, who put up with all my entrepreneurial craziness. And to all my real estate investors who make my real estate journey possible, especially Jim Balletta, Pete Collette, Jerry and Rosie Voelker, and Don Bergner for believing in me from day one. And to the folks at the DNAgency in Orlando, especially Angie Swenson and Mandy Tawbush, for helping me get this book to the finish line.

CONTENTS

INTRODUCTION

As I visit the 30+ mobile home communities that I own, I often wonder why the Great Recession of 2008-2009 hasn't ended for most Americans. For most people in the country, the economy is still struggling as decent paying jobs are scarce, and prices for many of the essentials – food, gas, energy, health care, education, etc. – are increasing steadily. As I look to the future, I only see the situation getting worse as the ridiculously partisan politicians (at all levels) accomplish nothing and keep the *status quo* of the "Rich Getting Richer" and letting everyone else fend for themselves. And if you look at the predictions for the most needed jobs over the next 5-10 years, 9 out of the top 10 pay $8-12/hour. Is this the new normal? It sure looks like it to me.

But there are two groups of investors making a lot of money in these difficult times. The first group gets a lot of press—the new tech entrepreneurs in Silicon Valley. The IPOs of Facebook, Twitter, etc. have minted thousands of new millionaires. I greatly admire these people as they have incredible vision and math and science skills I could only dream about. Most of these people are super achievers in the STEM categories—Science, Technology, Engineering, and Math. I firmly believe the STEM world will continue to prosper, and I encourage all young people to pursue those fields if they have the aptitude and passion for them. All three of my sons have a great aptitude for math and computer science, and I want to provide them every opportunity possible to increase their skills.

The problem is that the people with the aptitude and passion to succeed in the STEM fields consist of 15%–20% of the country. But what about everyone else, like myself, who hate math and have little understanding of how modern technology works (but love to use the stuff)—how are we going to succeed in this tough economy that may remain sluggish for years? Quite by accident, I stumbled into a field I call the *Main $treet Millionaires*

(M$Ms) that is also printing millionaires. These people, like myself, have made more money in the last four years than they have at any time in their career, and they have done it in an *Unconventional* manner – by providing quality, ethical, low cost goods and services that a majority of Americans need and can't get anywhere else. By providing these services, the M$M's are making a lot of money, but they are also helping a lot of people get services that they badly need. And the future for this field looks increasingly bright as well. But before I get to the M$M opportunity, let me show you how I stumbled into the field.

I grew up in a family that followed the advice of my Dad, who was a successful corporate guy who stayed at the same bank for thirty-five years. He preached the **Three G Program**—good grades (at a liberal arts college no less), good job (in corporate America), and good retirement (through a 401(k) plan). My Dad preached it because that's what made him successful in his time. However, I failed miserably at this program because my innate skills were much more suitable for entrepreneurism than corporate America. The problem was I didn't figure this out until I was thirty-two years old, when I took my first Myers-Briggs personality/skills test. The test results were a huge slap in the face to me—I came out as a strong entrepreneur. No wonder I liked to take risks, had to be the team leader, and seldom listened to authority. If I had known this sooner, it would've helped me avoid a lot of failures and heartache. But what I realized is that my "formal" education was actually a huge hindrance, not a help, on my path to becoming an M$M. I learned so little practical knowledge in all my years of school, it was pathetic. I should definitely be entitled to a refund!

Looking back on the last twenty years, it's been a crazy entrepreneurial ride. Starting from a net worth of $ 50,000 at age thirty, my family (my kids own a small part of all my deals) now has a net worth well into 8 figures derived from three different M$M businesses—financial services, affordable apartments, and mobile home communities. Here's a quick snapshot of my story:

Financial Services: 1992–2002
I ran a small broker-dealer (broker-dealers are responsible for supervising financial planners and helping them grow their businesses) that I grew from five employees and $1.2 million in gross dealer concessions (revenue) to more than $40 million and over fifty employees in five years before selling to a large national insurance company. I also bought a financial planning practice that I grew to over $100 million in assets under management before selling it in the early 2000s after I became completely disillusioned with Wall Street and the financial planning business.

Apartment Complexes: 2003–2006
I bought, rehabbed, and subsequently sold seven affordable housing apartment complexes in Orlando, FL ranging in size from 64 to 120 units. I had no intention of selling, but the prices got ridiculous and I had to sell, with sales totaling over $25 million. My timing was good on this, as six of the seven of the properties went into foreclosure within three years after I sold them.

Mobile Home Communities: 2007–Current
I bought, rehabbed, and sold six larger mobile home communities in North Carolina and Michigan, all of which were strong cash cows, for sales totaling over $40 million. People in the business thought I was crazy for selling, but I have reinvested the proceeds from the sales and now own 31 mobile home communities with just over 3,700 spaces with crazy cash flow. My company is now valued at $75 million, up from $15 million two years ago.

When I started my entrepreneurial journey, I believe I was like a majority of Americans:

- I was clueless about the exploding tech industry and had no skills to participate in it.
- I didn't have any idea how to buy, run, or own real estate.
- I had no accounting or tax background.

- I had no entrepreneurial training or mentors to study under.
- I had very limited sales skills.

Despite numerous failures (see the extensive list in Section 5, Biz Skillz #6), I discovered the M$M opportunity and am extremely fortunate to have been able to able to live the *Main Street Millionaire* lifestyle for the last fifteen-plus years. I work out of my house approximately twenty-five hours per week. I can take as much time off as I want, but I can also delve into my passion of doing real estate deals or other cash flow opportunities when the time is right. I have no board of directors and no equal partners. I have time to connect with friends, whether it is through being the fantasy football commissioner, being able to ride my mountain bike every Wednesday and Friday morning with friends, or having time to volunteer coaching youth basketball.

I know that money isn't the only source of happiness, but I can tell you that money can get you one of the most important gifts we have in this life—freedom! I am not necessarily speaking of political freedom (which we all take way too much for granted in this country) but more so of time freedom—having the financial security to do what you want, when you want. I am not the richest guy I know by far, but most people who meet me want my lifestyle. You don't need to be a billionaire like Trump to become an M$M and live the M$M lifestyle. You don't need a mansion or fancy cars. You just need to own cash-flowing M$M businesses and/or properties that provide you with an income that is at least 50% more than your expenses. Trust me, you will enjoy your life a lot more if you have ample free time to pursue your passions in life, because you have the peace of mind that being an M$M brings you!

I have two goals with this book: first, to provide some recognition for a lot of great businesspeople you may know little about, and second, to open your eyes to a tremendous business opportunity that *anyone can do*, even in this ugly economy, no matter how old you are and regardless of your past experience or education level. However, as I will teach you in this book, the old ways of doing things will not work! The Three G Program (good grades, good job, good retirement) doesn't work anymore for most Americans. And you can't save your way to prosperity anymore either, especially with interest rates at 0% for a long time. I do know you can become a *Main Street Millionaire* by helping a ton of people in the fastest-growing consumer segment get quality, affordable, and ethical services, because I have done it and I know lots of others who have done it as well. Let me teach you how.

SECTION 1

WELCOME TO THE UNITED STATES OF GUATEMALA

The U.S. Government tells us that the Great Recession ended a couple of years ago, but for most of the people in America it doesn't feel that way. To them, the "rich," and especially the top 1%, have benefitted enormously from the bailing out of the big banks, but Main Street has been 'left holding the bag' as wages have actually gone down for most of America over the last 30 years and day-to-day costs continue to rise. Here are a couple of quick facts to consider:

- The top 1% of Americans now own assets worth more than those held by the entire bottom 90%.
- The six Wal Mart heirs have a net worth that equals the entire net worth of the bottom 41% of American households combined.
- 83% of all stock market assets are held by the top 10% of the population.

The definition of "working poor" by the Working Poor Families Project is a family of four earning approximately $45,000 per year or less. Look below at the financial reality of a family of four in middle America where each spouse makes $10 per hour:

Gross Monthly Income:	**$3,465**
Social Security and Medicare	$250
Federal Taxes—5%	$175
State Taxes—3%	$105
Health Insurance (can't afford)	$ 0
401(k) Savings	<u>$ 0</u>
Net Take-Home:	**$2,935**
Monthly Rent	$900
Utilities (phone, cable, electricity, water and sewer, heat and air)	$180
Food (with food stamps)	$400
One Car Payment	$300
Car Insurance	$120
Gas	$250
Secondhand Clothing	$ 50
Minor Medical/Dental Costs	$100
Left After Necessities:	
Entertainment/Fun Expenses	*$285 Bones!*
College Savings	HA!
Retirement Savings	You're Kidding, Right?
Credit Card Debt	Skyrockets!

This scenario is truly horrifying, especially without health insurance and not saving a dime for college or retirement. These families live paycheck to paycheck, are one serious illness or job loss away from bankruptcy, and will have to work until they die because they will have no retirement savings. The sad thing is that their children have a 90% chance of falling into the "working poor" category when they become adults. We need to be honest—the American dream has become a myth for most of our country.

So how many people in the United States are categorized as "working poor"? According to the 2010 US Census data, *the number of "poor" and "working poor" in the United States totaled 146.4 million—48% of the population! And the Associated Press recently compiled a report that showed four out of five adults in America struggle with joblessness, near poverty or reliance on welfare for at least part of their lives.* And don't think the problem is just related to minorities, as hardships among whites is rising the fastest.

Mark my words—the number of "working poor" in America is only going to go up over the next ten years as millions more in the middle class tumble toward working poor status. In fact, I predict the number of poor and working poor is going to push towards 80% of the population over the next decade. Why do I predict this discouraging trend of moving towards becoming the United States of Guatemala? Four reasons: huge government and personal debt, the job market has changed permanently for the worse, the public education system is a failure in working poor communities, and costs for the basics continue to rise. Arianna Huffington's book *Third World America*, published in 2010 (she is a great entrepreneur as well, as evidenced by her selling the *Huffington Post* to AOL for $315 million—nice!) lays out the case for the United States becoming a third world country much better than I can. The only thing I disagree with in her book is that she was optimistic that this third world scenario can be avoided. I don't think so. Here is my quick version:

The Coin Has Run Out...

We all know we have 'way' overspent as a country. The federal government is technically broke and is an interest spike away from not being able to pay its debts. As of mid-2014, the federal deficit is over $17 trillion and is now equal to 100% of the economic output of the country. *Let's be clear: we will never pay this debt back. We are only talking about trying to control its upward spiral and pay the current interest payments.* What happens if short-term interest rates go back to historical norms of 3%–5% from the current 0.5%? All bets are off as the interest payments on the debt will rise from the current level of 11% of the federal budget to over 25%! That means significantly less money for every other federal program.

State governments have done a better job over the last couple years of cutting their spending, but the promises they have made to their current and retired employees in regard to pension and health care benefits are a huge problem that will manifest itself over the next five to ten years. Estimates are that state and local governments have a $1 trillion hole they will need to fill to keep those promises. I predict the state and local governments will threaten bankruptcy and/or go to court to get these promises reduced, which will push more seniors from a middle class retirement into a working poor retirement.

Every part of government needs to be cut drastically over the next twenty years (no, the problem won't be solved in a few years as the politicians like to promise), and the working poor will suffer the most as they depend on the government far more than the rich. The rich aren't affected by budget cuts—as police budgets are cut, they can install their own security systems or hire their own private security; massive cuts to public education are irrelevant to them, as most send their kids to private schools; and cuts to public transportation don't affect them because they have their own cars. The working poor, on the other hand, depend on the police to protect their neighborhoods, they can't afford private schools, and many rely on public transportation.

And personal debt is also still too high, even though people have scaled back since the Great Recession of 2008–2009:

- The average personal credit card debt still averages over $7,000 per person, but when you analyze only the cards that have an outstanding balance after 30 days (i.e., toss out the cards owned by the "rich" who pay off their cards every month), the average balance soars to over $15,000! The average interest rate for those people is 14.95%.

- The total of all student loan debt has surpassed $1 trillion as the average college grad has over $31,000 in student loans and $5,200 in credit card balances. And that's not all—parents' personal loan debt to cover college for their kids is now over $100 billion, which averages over $10,000 per college grad.

- 41% of Americans have less than $500 in savings...wow!

And lets be real about the tax system in America. It is heavily skewed to favor the top 20% of the country as there are great tax breaks for owning an expensive home, a corporate jet, a beach house, a yacht, etc. And the best tax break going is for hedge funds and private equity firms that get a 35% tax break because...they create so much value for the country. Really? Does the fact that the Top 25 hedge fund managers pulled down a combined $24.3 billion between them in 2013 justify a 35% tax break? We absolutely need a flat tax with no deductions for anyone. Unfortunately, the chances of that ever happening is also zero percent, because our crony capitalist politicians will never stop taking the corporate handouts offered to them.

The Job Market Is Still on Life Support...
The job market has improved of late, but it's still far from healthy. 10.5 million Americans are still out of work. A few more facts to consider:

- The manufacturing jobs that are "coming onshore" (back to America) are not nearly as good as the old manufacturing jobs that sustained our middle class. Most of these jobs average $12–$16 per hour and provide no pensions and significantly scaled-back health insurance.

Obviously these jobs are a blessing for those who are out of work, but it won't get them out of the working poor category and into the middle class like the old days.

- Of the total number of jobs created in 2010–2014, 76% paid between $8.92 and $14 per hour, well below the national average of $22.60 per hour. The Bureau of Labor Statistics just published their job outlook through 2020. The report found that 63% of all jobs to be created will require a high school degree or less—i.e., a lot more $8–14 per-hour jobs. Winner, winner, chicken dinner!

The Public Education System Doesn't Work for the Working Poor...

- While there are some fine K–12 public education systems in affluent areas of the country, the United States ranks twenty-first in science and twenty-fifth in math compared to other high schools in the thirty largest industrialized countries.

- Almost 25% of U.S. kids never graduate from high school, which is a direct ticket to working poor status for the rest of their lives. The dropout rate for minorities is close to 50%.

- In the U.S., 2.2 million people were in jails or prisons, which is five times greater than any other developed country in the world. The privately run (yes, most states don't run their own prisons) prisons are some of the biggest political contributors in the country.

But Costs for the Basics Are Still Rising...

- $3.50/gallon is the new normal for gas prices.

- Health insurance costs went up by 75% from 2003 to 2014, with the cost of family coverage now over $14,000 per year. As a small-business owner in North Carolina, my carrier jacked up my premiums by 29% and forced me to take less coverage even though we had little change in our health costs from the prior year.

- College tuition costs at public universities have increased over 30% in just the last four years and 538% since 1985! And where is the tuition rising fastest? At universities where the top administrators are paid the most. These are the universities spend ridiculous amounts on the useless buildings and big-time football programs while also hiring the most part-time, cheap faculty so they can get paid more.

One potential solution for soaring college costs is occurring in Indiana at Purdue University, now led by the former governor Mitch Daniels, which has frozen tuition for the last three years. Daniels said "the freeze turned out not to be terribly hard to do. Instead of asking our students' families to adjust their budgets to our desired spending, let's adjust our spending to their reduced budgets." The college "bubble" that has developed over the last thirty years will be the biggest bust over the next five to ten years.

And Richie Rich Just Keeps Getting...Richer
The result of this mess that we are in as a country is that the gap between the rich and the working poor is wider than ever in our country's history and is going to widen further in the decade ahead:

- Middle class families' net worth plunged by 39% from 2007-2014 and now stands at 1992 levels! Meanwhile, the top 10% of households in the U.S. still earned a minimum of $349,000 in 2014.

- The top 20% of wealthy Americans now own 84% of all the country's wealth!

- The richest 1% of households in America now have a net worth 225 times greater than the average American household!

- The *average* chief executive officer in America makes 475 times what the average American worker makes (versus twenty-two times for British CEOs and eleven times for Japanese CEOs).

I am not an economist, so I can't predict when or how the issues listed above will affect our economy, but it's easy to see that they won't help. And I don't pretend to have the answers on how to fix the problems, as I'm not sure there are any viable solutions. What I do know is that over the next few years, I see two distinctly separate economies emerging in the United States—the daily struggle of the working poor and the insulated bubble of the rich. The problem will be magnified by demographics as the population over 65 in America will soar by over 100% from today's numbers, which will cause Medicare and Social Security spending to soar and thus requiring all other government programs to be slashed in a big way. If you are under the age of 55, you need to expect the following:

- Social Security will be 25% less than current amounts and if you make more than $60,000 in retirement you will probably receive nothing;

- Medicare will provide a fraction of what is currently covered and the average couple will need a minimum of $250,000 saved prior to retirement just for health care costs!

So I know what you are thinking now: "thanks for the giant buzz kill," and "what the heck do I do now because I don't have the STEM skills discussed in the introduction?" Do I give up and accept a significantly lower standard of living? Do I refocus my pursuits to the "new" American dream of getting on the disability program? Of course not. You may think I am joking, but the number of Americans receiving a monthly check for a disability is almost 8.5 million—up more than 60% in the last ten years, though that fund is scheduled to run dry in 2016, throwing even more people into the "working poor" category. In fact, I believe that for those who are willing to change their mind-set and think outside the box, the next ten years will provide some of the greatest financial and entrepreneurial opportunities ever. The problem is that the old ways of doing things won't work anymore. You need to start thinking like a *Main Street Millionaire*!

SECTION 2

THE M$M OPPORTUNITY

*You will get all you want in life, if you help enough other
people get what they want.*
~ Zig Ziglar

A *Main Street Millionaire* (M$M) is an entrepreneur who
wants to control his/her own financial future by owning small
to medium-sized businesses in his/her community that focus on
providing *quality, affordable, and ethical* services to the largest
and fastest-growing consumer segment in the United States—
the working poor. An M$M makes their money by helping
others get what they desperately need at affordable prices and
by treating their customers with respect and dignity. A true M$M
may have some formal education (a community college degree
is usually sufficient), but he/she surely has lots of street smarts
and experience in the community. Let's compare an M$M to a
Wall Street millionaire:

Main $treet Millionaire

1. Owns small to medium-sized businesses ($100k to $15
   million in revenue) that focus on providing quality, ethical
   services to working poor.
2. Works his/her ass off, especially in the early years.
3. Has no Board of Directors.
4. Focuses on his/her passion.
5. Enjoys unlimited time off after getting established.

6. Never retires.

7. Has no stock market investments.

8. Builds a small, close-knit family of employees.

9. Has time for mountain biking/Fantasy Football.

10. Is humble and cool "about the coin."

Wall Street/Corporate Millionaire

1. Climbs the corporate ladder.

2. Grinds it out 60-80+ hour per week.

3. Does lots of corporate travel all over the world.

4. Puts up with corporate B.S.

5. Gets 4 weeks of vacation, but non-stop checking of cell phone on vacation is mandatory.

6. Gets forced out at age 55.

7. Has a retirement that is 100% dependent on the stock market.

8. Is a die-hard Republican and believes that "tax cuts" are the answer to every problem.

9. Plays golf /and or shoots skeet at the "club."

10. Lives for the status to impress others.

The opportunity to become a Wall Street millionaire is limited to the few who possess either the STEM skills or the AF skills— accounting and finance—derived from an expensive education. They also have to put up with huge amounts of stress and very little control over their destiny, and they need to be able to brown nose with the best of them. The M$M opportunity, on the other hand, is available to anyone willing to work hard, regardless of age, prior experience, or education level and it allows you to control your own destiny

Prior to the Great Recession, the old Main Street Millionaires used to be the department store owners, the local bank president, the upscale restauranteur, the luxury homebuilder, and the new-car dealer. But Main Street has changed rapidly in the last five years. The department store has been replaced by the pawnshop. The bank president is now the local branch manager making $40K per year. The upscale restaurant owner is still struggling – with most being replaced by the fast-food franchisee. The luxury homebuilder is just getting through bankruptcy and has been replaced by an affordable rental housing landlord. The new car dealer exists, but his/her profits come from the "buy here/pay here" department that focuses on the "working poor" customers.

I see the new *M$Ms* having terrific opportunities in five industries that provide affordable, quality services to the rapidly-growing consumer segment known as the "working poor" in America.

1. **Finance**—With over 50% of Americans unable to get any credit and priced out by most of the banks – which charge ridiculous bounced-check fees as high as $40 – the pawnshops are filling a vital role. Most people who watch the pawnshop reality shows think their main business is buying and selling exotic items. However, the largest service of the pawnshops is about providing small loans (the average loan is $100), check cashing, and tax prep services to the working poor and, increasingly, the middle class. The pawnshops that focus on the financial services model have unlimited opportunity over the next decade.

2. **Affordable Rental Housing**—Most of the custom home builders are struggling back from bankruptcy, but the new home market is a still far below 2007 levels. Whether it is individual homes, apartments, or mobile home communities, the demand for quality, affordable rental housing is booming.

3. **Fast Food**—Chick-fil-A is the hottest fast-food franchise going. A fast-growing chain herein the Southeast called Bojangles' has Chick-fil-A in its sights.

4. Retail—Walmart obviously started the trend here. The dollar-type stores (Dollar Tree, etc.) have become a mainstay in the retail world, with almost ten thousand stores in the United States from all the chains. Aaron's Rents and Rent-A-Center are also booming as a majority of Americans can't afford to purchase furniture or appliances outright anymore. I throw the car dealers under retail as well. The used-car dealers, like Drive Time - that can provide on-the-spot financing - are booming. Note that all the big car dealerships in any town now have a "buy here/pay here" department like Drive Time. The "used" goods sellers, like used clothing or used tires are doing huge business.

5. Senior Care: With the explosion of baby boomers now retiring, the number of working poor seniors will skyrocket over the next ten to twenty years as Medicare will have to be cut and Social Security will have to be adjusted downward. The demand for affordable senior apartments, home health care, and affordable assisted living will explode.

And guess what? All of these industries are dying for workers to fill jobs, none of which require a college degree. And if you have sales skills, you can write your own ticket. A prime example is my buddy, Jeremy. He is the manager of a nice pawnshop in Durham, North Carolina, owned by Bob Moulton (see below). He never went to college. He bounced around a couple of other retail jobs, but along the way he really sharpened his sales skills. And now he's clearing $100K managing a pawn shop! He has a big need to hire people immediately with a decent work ethic and some sales skills. If you're unemployed, you need to look at these industries.

Who are some of today's *Main Street Millionaires* who are thriving?

Financial:

- **John Thedford** started in the pawnshop business, working in the trenches of a store in the early 1990s (who was thinking about it then?) and began buying and setting up more shops. He ended up with sixty-seven stores and sold them to a bigger corporate pawn company for a cool $115 million in 2007! You need to get his book, *Smart Moves Management*. He has helped revolutionize the pawn shop business by significantly upgrading thestores and stressing customer service. Most of his entry-level employees made over $15 per hour!

- **Bob Moulton,** from Raleigh, North Carolina, was trained in the pawn business by his mother, who had her own store. He now owns seven pawnshops in North Carolina and grosses over $7 million per year. He has been instrumental in changing the face of the pawn industry with bigger, nicer stores. Bob was named 2011 National Pawnbroker of the Year.

Affordable Housing:

- **Milt Shiffman**, a former doctor, and his son Gary started Sun Communities in 1981. The firm is now publicly traded and owns 155 affordable housing mobile home communities (definitely not trailer parks) throughout the United States.

- **Carlos Vaz** is a young guy who recognized the downturn in the apartment business. In 2009, he started buying older apartment complexes in Texas that needed rehab and had been foreclosed on after the recent meltdown. He mastered the art of raising money from other people, and his Conti Apartments now owns almost four thousand units and he has "flipped" a few other complexes for sizable gains. Most important, he puts a lot of money into making properties that were "run into the ground" into quality, safe, and affordable places for families to live.

Fast Food:

- **Jack Fulk,** from Charlotte, North Carolina, started a low-end fast-food chain called Bojangles' (you need to try their Bo-Berry Biscuits!) and grew it to over 350 stores before selling it for millions.

- **Truett Cathy** founded Chick-fil-A in 1986 and has grown it to over 1,600 stores. Chik-fil-A is known for its great chicken sandwiches (containing real chicken) and for being closed on Sundays – to give employees a chance to go to church and have a day off.

Retail:

- **K. R. Perry** started the Dollar Tree stores in 1986 and has taken the company public. Dollar Tree now has over four thousand stores.

- **Charles Loudermilk, Sr.,** founded Aaron's Rental Centers with $500 back in the 1960s and now the chain has over 1,500 stores.

- **Ernest Garcia** founded Ugly Duckling car dealerships in 1991. After many years of struggling, he finally hit on the "buy here/pay here" strategy that appeals to the working poor. He renamed the firm Drive Time in 2002, and the company now has over eighty dealerships across the country that employ over 2,300 people. Their annual revenue is over $800 million.

Senior Care:

- **Mal Mixon** acquired Invacare, the world's leading manufacturer of wheelchairs and home healthcare equipment, in 1979, and has grown it from $19 million in sales to over $2 billion.

OK, stop! I know what you are thinking: these guys have made millions by preying on the working poor, just as Gary Rivlin portrays in his book, *Broke USA: From Pawnshops to Poverty— How the Working Poor Became Big Business* (2010). I totally disagree. While Rivlin's book makes some great points about the shysters in the mortgage business during the subprime debacle, I think he misses the point that the new M$M's mentioned above are providing *quality, affordable, and ethical* services to the largest and fastest-growing group of consumers in the United States—the working poor. The pawnshops run by Thedford and Moulton are really nice, clean, big stores providing access to loans and check cashing that is nonexistent for the working poor. The Shiffman family provides very nice, affordable housing to thousands of people around the country. These communities are as nice as most high-end apartment complexes. Moreover, all of these guys together are employing thousands of workers. Are they making money? Of course; this is America. Do we begrudge Nike or Nordstrom for making money selling overpriced brand names? Or the big banks, even though, in my opinion, they gouge consumers with their pricing?

Zig Ziglar, the legendary motivational speaker put the key to any business success as follows: "help others get what they want and you will be successful." This is simple, but so true, and it applies perfectly to the M$M businesses. Whether it's clean, safe, affordable housing or access to loans with great customer service, this axiom applies.

However, like any other business in this highly competitive economy, you will not succeed for long if your M$M business provides a shoddy product or sub-par service. The following table outlines the differences between M$Ms and predators:

	M$Ms	Predators
Consumer Loans	Clean, professional-looking pawnshops.	Payday lenders who charge 400%-plus in interest and tend to get clients in a vicious cycle.
Affordable Rental Housing	Investors who own clean and safe properties and reinvest in them with regard for the residents' safety welfare.	Slumlords who suck all the money out of their properties.
Fast Food	Clean, new stores with healthy menu choices.	Rundown buildings with greasy fare and no choices.
Retail	Clean stores with great customer service and reasonable fees.	Dirty stores with poor customer service; unethical used-car dealers.
Senior Care	Clean living units and outstanding customer service.	Unclean living units, disregard for residents, poor employee training.
Education	Low-cost, high-content webcast providers.	"Adult" education providers that put a hard sell on the working poor to sign up for big loans (paid for by the government) they can't afford.

There is a clear distinction between hardworking M$M's who reinvest in their businesses and those who don't care about their clients or properties and fail to reinvest in them. I know a mobile home park owner that lost 28 parks to the banks over the last couple years because he was a greedy slumlord. Fortunately for me, I bought 8 of those parks for incredibly low prices and have turned them all around from being "trailer parks" to mobile home "communities."

Again, the great thing about the M$M opportunity is that anyone can participate. A four-year college degree usually isn't required. The key requirements to becoming an M$M are a willingness to work hard, an upbeat personality, and a willingness to learn. What I've laid out in the ensuing chapters is a simple path to follow that will allow anyone a shot at an M$M opportunity. Remember, the Three Gs program doesn't work anymore. You need a new set of 'skillz' to succeed. Let me show you!

SECTION 3

THE M$M FOUNDATION

In order to become an M$M, you need to have a solid foundation from which you can launch yourself into success. The M$M personal foundation is not taught anywhere in the American education system so you need to do it on your own. Some people will view this information as hokey and not that important, but I am living proof that the foundation works. You need to integrate it into your daily life and I promise you will become much happier and you will achieve the success you've always wanted. Just remember the acronym – CASHFLOW.

C – Conquer the Fear

I think one of the biggest things holding people back from success is succumbing to the fear of what other people think of them. When I grew up, the pressure to conform to the 3G's program - good grades, good job, good retirement - was huge. I came from a "good" middle class family so I was expected to toe the line. Because of that pressure, I rebelled. There were a few times when I got into serious trouble as a teenager (throwing a rock through a police car window, jumping off a pretty high bridge for $50, waking up in the hospital from an alcohol binge, etc). Oh yes, I was a risk taker from early on – just not the right kind. My Dad told me a couple of times that I had "ruined the family name." I was expected to conform to society's norms of good behavior and when I didn't, I felt their wrath and quickly slipped back into "fear" mode of worrying what others thought of me.

I continued to live in this "fear" as I went to law school and then into corporate America. I took that path because that is "what I was supposed to do." As I got older and I really immersed myself into reading books such as Napoleon Hill's **Think and Grow Rich** and Rhonda Byrne's **The Secret,** I realized that I had to break free from the fear of worrying what others thought of me. One of the main reasons I moved from Wisconsin to Florida in my mid-30's was to break away from that pressure and fear. And once I broke free and finally became truly happy and stopped worrying about what others thought of me, the success started to pour in. The success definitely wasn't overnight and a lot of hard work went into it, but I firmly believe removing this roadblock was a huge factor in my success.

A – Attitude of Gratitude

I try to wake up every morning and thank God for my many blessings and really live life with an attitude of gratitude. The people I see in my life that are truly successful are the ones who are down to earth and thankful for everything they have.

One of those people is a friend of mine named Marti Hampton. Marti grew up in extreme poverty in the rural mountains of western North Carolina. Her father was an alcoholic and her parents divorced when she was 13. Her home life was so toxic she was forced to move out at age 15 and lived at the local YMCA. The rule was you were supposed to be 18 to live at the YMCA, but her circumstances forced her to become a salesperson at a young age and she talked her way in. She was kicked out of the YMCA 8 months later for drinking alcohol. She was forced into living in a boarding house and somehow made it through high school.

Right after high school, she "escaped" to Florida and got an administrative job working for a group of successful Jewish brokers selling land around Ocala, FL to "southerners" as they called them.

Marti's big break came when the brokers were struggling to communicate with the "southerners" because of cultural differences. Marti knew exactly how to do that because she was one. She soon became a success in that office, which led to success selling real estate in Miami, Atlanta, and for the last 20 years or so in Raleigh. She is now one of the most successful realtors in the country! She runs the local Remax office and has been the #1 Remax office in the country several times, and is always one of the top one or two offices in North Carolina amongst all realtors. Marti is a shining example of living with an attitude of gratitude. She believes strongly, as I do, that she is divinely guided and that there is a divine plan for her life. When you have that mindset and belief, you can't help but be grateful for everything in your life.

I firmly believe that nothing will change your outlook or make you happier than living with an attitude of gratitude. Too many people focus on their problems instead of their blessings. I am not a very religious person, but I am spiritual. I am a big fan of Joel Osteen, the pastor at Lakewood Community Church in Houston and the author of several best selling books and an incredible entrepreneur in his own right. Joel is a strong proponent of living with an attitude of gratitude and he says "that by living this way, not only will you thank God for what he's already done in your life, you start thanking Him for what he will do in the future. You thank Him for the new doors he will open for you and the new people he will bring into your life."

S – See It to Believe It
One of the great gifts my parents gave me was that they

really believed in positive thinking and visualization. They had gone to a weekend course on these topics and my Dad really believed it changed his life. I remember sitting down with my parents in my teens and recording a 15-20 minute tape of my own positive affirmations. Once I was done recording, I would go to a quiet place and listen to the affirmations and visualize them coming true. I didn't really understand why I was doing this, but it has paid enormous dividends for me and I am a strong believer in it today. I lost focus of this process when I went to college, but I picked it up again in my mid-20's. I used to carry around a small index card in my wallet with all of my goals and positive thoughts. I would take it out a couple of times a day and close my eyes and repeat them in my head. My main two professional goals were to be a financial services millionaire and to be a real estate millionaire. I didn't even really know what that meant back then, but I knew I wanted it. Within 10 years both goals came true!

As I have become more successful, I have found a couple times in the last few years where I get lazy and stop working on my goals and affirmations. When that happens, I tend to plateau with my success and start sliding into the bad habit of worrying more. But God always finds something or someone to wake me up to get back into the process. The most recent time came about a year or so ago. I had become more than comfortable in my lifestyle and found myself skipping my affirmations and visualizations more often. Then I walked into the office of one of our new managers, Erica Barr, at one of our mobile home parks near Charlotte. On her wall was a collage of all of her dreams and goals, the first among them was owning a Jeep Wrangler.

I used to have a similar collage when I was younger so I immediately was intrigued. I asked her about it and it led into her telling me about her life story. She grew up in a lower middle class home in the Miami area. Her parents divorced when she was young and her mother remarried.

Her step Dad was super strict and didn't allow them to watch TV or have friends. Hurricane Andrew wiped out their house in 1992 so they lived in a small trailer in their back yard for over five years while her step Dad rebuilt the house by himself. Things got so bad at home that she left at age 15, dropping out of high school in the 9th grade, and was basically homeless and living on the streets for several years. She bounced around lower-paying jobs, but managed to get her GED.

Erica had her first child at age 18, but it came from a very difficult relationship. She was on her own for several years after that and developed a very strong 'survivor' mentality. She was a hard worker that just couldn't catch a break. She had her second child from another relationship but that didn't work out either. She got a job in the property management business and started to flourish only to lose her job when the owner sold the property. Somewhat out of desperation, she ended up at our park. Not only was I extremely moved by her story, I was even more impressed by her positive, upbeat spirit.

This girl has been through way more hardships that I could possibly imagine, but she acted as if life was great. She said the book *The Secret* had changed her life and she was now a firm believer in positive thinking and visualization despite all of her setbacks. Erica has now become one of our best managers and through her hard work, she has earned pay raises and bonuses that allowed her to buy her first Jeep Wrangler!

H – Happiness is a Secret

Like Erica our manager, I have always been a fan of the book *The Secret* by Rhonda Byrne. I strongly urge everyone to read it or read it again if they haven't done so in a while. The book is a simple read and its greatness is that it takes old ideas and makes them new again. While the book certainly has its share of critics, I found its central theme of the law of attraction and its focus on the importance of gratitude and visualization to be very true with my life. I think it's a great guide for establishing happiness in anyone's life.

One of the themes of the book I really enjoy is the focus on abundance. I try to live my life with a spirit of abundance as much as I can. I firmly believe that the more you help other people, the more your life will be blessed. I have seen so many people in business try to screw other people for nickels instead of focusing on the bigger picture and trying to make it an abundant deal that is a win/win for both parties. Abundance is about positivity and happiness. Screwing other people over nickels is about negativity and leads to misery.

Elon Musk, the owner of Tesla electric cars, is a guy I admire a lot because he is brilliant and a risk taker. He just released all of his company patents, which are worth millions if not billions of dollars, to the public because he is so passionate in his belief that electric cars will save the planet. He wants to share his knowledge with the world in the hope that someone else will take that knowledge and make the world a better place. That is abundance!

F – Forward Progress

I am a big believer in always moving forward and rarely looking back. I think it keeps me young as I am always excited about the next adventure coming in my life. I try to balance looking forward with living in the moment as I really want to enjoy the journey, but I rarely look back on my life. The only time I really look back on my life is to thank God for my blessings or to laugh about some experience. I don't hold grudges, I don't beat myself up for past mistakes, and I forgive people easily. I think it's the only way to live as I have seen my brother, my mother, my ex-wife, and way too many others lose big portions of their lives to this negative energy.

I recently went to my 30th high school reunion and realized that most of my classmates were still living in the past. It was like a time warp. Most had never lived further than two hours away from where they grew up. Most still had the same friends, boring mid-level corporate jobs that were going nowhere, lived vicariously through their kids' meager athletic achievements, and generally did the same things all the time. But what I realized is that they were normal and I was very different. Most people would never take the risks I have: moved to different states, jumped out of airplanes, met amazing new people, and fully grasped the adventure of life. Most people don't want others to succeed. I want everyone to succeed.

I owe a big credit to my friend Mateen Chaudhry who has really propelled me forward recently. He came into my life a couple years ago because he really believed in the mobile home parks. He had a great career in investment banking in Tokyo, Hong Kong, and New York, but he was really burned out by it. He had seen things in the capital markets that I never had, and he strongly believed that my business was ripe for big growth. I was stuck in a bit of a comfort zone at the time. I was making great money, not working a lot, and generally being complacent. He shook me out of my comfort zone and made me look forward again. He put me in front of numerous investors who love the mobile home park concept. Now we are pushing forward in a big way and have doubled our business in a little over a year.

L – Like Yourself First

When I was a young child, my mother made me repeat the phrase "I like myself" ten times each night before I went to bed. I never really understood why she did that, but I did get it years later as I realized it gave me the basis for self-confidence. What I learned is that people who don't like themselves first have a very difficult time being successful in any type of relationship, whether it be personal or business. I think the biggest key to "liking yourself" is accepting yourself for who you are, which means knowing and understanding all of your strengths and all of your weaknesses. Since we tend to attract people who are like us in both personal and business relationships, once we have a good concept of who we are, we can play to our strengths and also try to improve our weaknesses. By playing to our strengths, we become more confident because we have better chances for success. But we also need to continually work on our weaknesses to make sure they don't cause the success to go away.

The opposite of playing to your strengths is trying to be something you are not. For example, I tried really hard to fit into corporate America because that's what I thought I was supposed to do. While I could fake it pretty well, I knew deep inside that something wasn't right. I couldn't play the political game well (a weakness), but I knew I was a strong leader (a strength) and would do whatever it took to succeed (another strength), even if it meant doing the lowliest of jobs. When I took the Briggs Myers test and found out I had strong entrepreneurial tendencies, I finally understood who I was. My strengths were the ability to take calculated risks and the ability to lead a team, which are two of the most important ingredients in being a successful entrepreneur.

O – Obstacles are Opportunities in Disguise

A couple years ago I was having lunch with one of my friends, Robbie Brafford. Robbie is one of the funniest, happiest people I know. He had been a local homebuilder and had flourished in the early 2000's, but got caught holding some lots and unfinished houses in 2008-09 and was really struggling with the debts from those deals, like most home builders during that time. He was forced to shut down his business and take a corporate job with one of his friends, who was in the used tire business, in order to keep paying his debts. (At the time, I didn't even know there was such as business). He was being forced to do a lot of corporate travel and he was helping install a software program at various offices throughout the country. Robbie is a natural salesman, so installing software was not his passion, but he needed the job. He told me that day at lunch that the prior day when he boarded his plane, he was really hoping that it crashed because his life was so miserable. I know he wasn't 100% serious, but I was shocked that he had gotten so depressed. I had been trying to convince him for a year or so that he needed to consider filing bankruptcy on his prior business, but he was too proud to do it and just didn't feel it was right.

After hearing and seeing his hurt, I decided I had to take action so I made him contact a great bankruptcy attorney that I know, George Oliver from New Bern, NC. Robbie finally called George and it turned out that he was a college classmate of Robbie's and they had hung together several times. Flash forward two years later and George had worked his magic and had gotten Robbie out of his debts for pennies on the dollar. Finally freed from his financial worries, the old Robbie came back and the doors started to open. He got along really well with one of the most influential people in the company (who happened to be my brother-in-law's brother – talk about a small world!) who got him out of the software installation and into sales where he belonged. I now call Robbie the $5 Million Man because he is crushing that mark every year in sales for the company. He is having more success than he ever did in the home-building industry. Robbie's obstacles were really opportunities in disguise, he just had to recognize them that way. And as it turns out, the used-tire business is a fantastic M$M business! Their primary end customers are the "working poor" who can't afford new tires.

The bottom line is that if you are ever going to achieve true success, you have to experience failure first. Although failure is gut wrenchingly difficult at times, you need to learn to accept it, get back on your feet, and become a stronger person from it. Those obstacles in your path are just opportunities in disguise.

I have failed almost too many times to count. I failed miserably at my first job in the financial services business because I had no idea on how to sell. I failed the bar exam twice. I went through a messy divorce. I was in some very tight places in my first few deals where I was close to losing hundreds of thousands of dollars. And I have also had personal obstacles to overcome. One of my best friends growing up, who was a quadriplegic, was "standing up" in my wedding. He was the life of the party at the reception, but he died in his sleep that night. Within a span of six months in late 2007 and early 2008, I lost my Mom to cancer, my Dad had a couple of mini-strokes and lost a lot of his cognitive functions (thank God he is still alive today), and I had to end my relationship with my brother, who was my best friend, because after my Dad and I spent almost $200,000 of our own money putting him through numerous trips to rehab, I realized his alcoholism had become so destructive that the only thing that was going to save him was going to jail.

And I am sure I will have more obstacles to overcome. But I will dig deep and I will bounce back!

W - What Are You Waiting For

When I do my seminars, I hold up a $100 bill near the beginning and say "who wants $100?" I then sit there in silence for a couple moments and repeat it again. "Who wants $100?" I start to hear shouts from the crowd saying "I do, I do" but no one moves. I repeat it again, "Who wants $100?" The crowd starts getting noisy and finally, after five or ten minutes, someone finally gets it and runs up and takes the $100 bill. I do the same exercise near the end of the seminar and I almost get tackled in the rush to get the $100.

The point of the exercise is that you have to learn overcome your fears and insecurities and take action! Taking action usually requires taking a risk and our society, especially our education system, so discourages us from taking any type of risk that for the small percentage of people who finally overcome their fears and do so, the upside benefits are enormous. In the real estate business, I see so many guys who will analyze a deal to death and try to find something wrong with it so they don't have to take a risk. In business, every sale or deal will have its problems. The key is to understand what your downside risk is, and if it's acceptable, pull the trigger and get the deal done.

The internal motto that I came up with for my firm, Affordable Communities Group, LLC, I took from several underdog sports teams – "Why Not Us?" We implemented the motto and decided to take action. Two years ago we were a $15 million company doing $2.5 million in annual rents. Now we are a $75 million company doing $10 million in annual rents. I now ask my Chief Operations Officer and my business partner for the last 13 years, Chris Barry, who is a huge reason for our success, why can't we be a $100 million company? Why can't we go public one day? Many other people have done it, Why not us?

As the legendary Steve Jobs once said, "Remembering that I will be dead soon is the most important tool I've ever encountered to help me make the big choices in my life." I also like what the rapper 2 Chainz says in one of his songs, "I don't fear death or dyin', I only fear never tryin'." An even simpler way to look at it comes from one of the actor Matt Damon's characters who says, "In order to change something, it only takes 20 seconds of courage." Learning to overcome your fears and take action is a huge key to achieving any level of success.

SECTION 4

M$M MONEY SKILLZ

Happiness is not in the possession of money,
but rather in the joy of making it.
~ Franklin Roosevelt

In my opinion, it is appalling that most people are so *stupid* when it comes to financial matters, and no, I don't think *stupid* is too strong a word. I have many friends whom I consider successful and smart who have no clue about the financial products they were sold or what to do with them. My dad spent thirty-five years in banking but has avery limited knowledge of any other financial matters except his company's stock, which was not a bad thing while the stock was doing great from 1983 to 2007, but it hasn't been pretty since 2008 when the stock is still down 40% from its highs and the dividend was slashed by 95%! Why did he have such a limited knowledge? That's because he was never taught anything about financial matters in school. Not in high school. Not in college. Not in grad school. It's an American tragedy. Let's see, I really need this biology class, even though I hate science, or this trigonometry class, even though I hate math, but God forbid if they teach me any practical realities about money and finance. God forbid they teach me something that will make me money!

One thing I will tell you with certainty is that you will be happier with money. Poverty is miserable. A recent study conducted by Princeton University economist Angus Deaton and famed psychologist Daniel Kahneman found that $75,000 per year was the *minimum* magic number for happiness. People who make that amount or more consider themselves happier than those making less than $75,000. I think the number is $100,000. Remember, money is definitely not the only thing that will make you happy, but having more money can give you the incredible gift of time freedom to pursue your life's passions.

It is alarming when you read through some of the recent reports on the woeful state of Americans and their personal finances. Here are a few of the stats:

- Fifty-four percent of American workers have less than $25,000 in retirement savings.

- Sixty percent of workers over the age of 55 have less than $100,000 saved for retirement. Even with Social Security, they will have to drastically scale back their lifestyle in retirement or work until they are 80.

- More than 25% of Americans making over $100K in household income didn't think they could come up with $2,000 in cash.

A recent story on CNNMoney.com highlighted a couple who were in their early forties, had $225K in annual household income, $300K in 401(k) accounts, and $0 in savings. Worse, they hit a few unexpected expenses and had $20K in credit card balances and had to borrow from their 401(k) to put on a new roof. Think about it—they are making $225K, in the top 15% of all households in America, and they have no liquid savings. Nada.

The first step toward becoming a M$M is to master the basics of money. I have detailed the seven most important M$M Money Skillz that you must know to have a chance at becoming an M$M!

SECTION 4 § CHAPTER 1

LIVE IN THE BASEMENT AS LONG AS YOU CAN

If you master only one thing about personal finance, I hope it is the age-old adage of "spend less than you make." Wow—what a concept, yet a vast majority of Americans disregard this rule in all aspects of their financial lives. M$Ms are scrappers with regard to their personal finances, as well as their business and real estate investments (see Sections 5 and 6), not wasteful consumers like the rest of America. I really like a majority of what Clark Howard and Dave Ramsey preach in regard to living within your means and reducing personal debt (I disagree with their belief in the stock market). I like to frame the discussion in terms of C-A-S-H-F-L-O-W. It doesn't matter if we're talking about business or real estate investments or your personal finances: CASH FLOW—having more revenue than expenses—is the key to becoming a *Main Street Millionaire*. Guess where positive CASH FLOW goes? In your pocket. Trust me when I say *you do not want to have negative CASH FLOW* in your personal finances, business, or real estate investments. Below are the CASH FLOW basics:

C – Cut the cards. You only need one credit card and you MUST pay it off each month! No transferring balances, opening multiple cards, or just swiping your card for a $4 latte, cigarettes, etc.

A – Accumulate cash. Start *now*. You need at least *eighteen months'* worth of living expenses in an FDIC-insured savings, money market or certificate of deposit (CD). The old rule of six months doesn't apply in this rocky economy. You are going to want this peace of mind whether you are starting your own business or entering volatile corporate America.

S – Study cost effectively. Your goal must be to have the least amount of education debt (it may not be college) possible, *preferably $0,* when you graduate. You don't want to be anchored with $50-100k of college debt that you can't even get rid of by filing bankruptcy.

This debt will put huge limits on what you can do with your life. Student loans are cancer!

H – Home entertainment rules. Scale back eating out, movies, concerts, and sporting events. Netflix is way cheaper than going out and sporting events are sometimes easier to see on TV. Stay home and save a lot of cash! Don't be afraid to brown-bag it at work when you are young. Eating out is a huge cash drain.

F – Flash is trash. No Jivin' with the Jones'; they're bankrupt now, anyway! The bling needs to go; buy knock-offs that look good without spending the bucks. Buy groceries in bulk at BJ's or Sam's Club.

Shop at T.J. Maxx, Marshall's or other discount stores. No phat $40K Audi with an $800-a-month payment. No charging vacations without a clue how to pay for them. No $15K birthday party for your seven-year old. *Nobody cares!* Don't look like a fool. Learn to avoid the instant gratification impulse. You'll have plenty of time to enjoy the perks when you become a *Main Street Millionaire*.

L – Live in the basement as long as possible. Keeping your housing/renting costs low is a great way to save some coin in your late teens and early twenties.

Getting some home-cooked meals and your laundry done once in a while aren't bad perks either.

O – Obtain a bankable skill for the least amount of money possible. A bankable skill is one that leads directly to a job—sales, accounting, tax prep, engineering, hair stylist, nail technician, real estate investor, etc. No more wasting huge amounts of money on worthless liberal arts, history, art, philosophy, or political science majors. And please stay away from "adult" education rip-offs that advertise an easy degree in your spare time and take your money. You need to have a much better focus (for sure by age 20) on the education you need.

W – Work your a** off...especially when you're young. Between the ages of 18-40, you have tons of energy, so you need to have your *Main $treet Millionaire* plan in place and stay focused on it. You can still have fun, but keep your priorities focused on the plan!

Working your *Main $treet Millionaire* plan does require some sacrifices—everything you do must take into account CASH FLOW. I live on less than 50% of my monthly cash flow from my real estate and business investments. I always keep a minimum cash balance of three years' worth of living expenses. I have my kids' educations paid for (not sure if it will be traditional college). I haven't carried a credit card balance in twenty years. Below is my recommendation for income allocation after taxes:

50% - Needs: Includes shelter (rent/mortgage payment), groceries, utilities, transportation, insurance, etc.

20% - Entertainment: Includes eatingout, movies, sporting events, etc.

20% - **Savings & Investment:** Includes adding to liquid savings, investing in a business or real estate, 401(k) contributions up to the company's 401 (k) match, pension contributions (see Money Skillz #4 below), or extra payments on a mortgage.

10% - **Charity:** I believe it's critical to give to others who are less fortunate. Put it in the budget.

If you analyze a $4,000/month take-home pay, $2,000 goes to needs, $800 to entertainment, $800 to savings and investment, and $400 to charity. If you can't conform to this allocation, you need to scale back your lifestyle.

M$M Star Tips

Live Large on Less

Below are 7 ways to live large on less money:

1. Buy all watches, jewelry, TV's, video games, etc. at a pawn store – name brands for less than 50% of retail.

2. Buy your designer clothes at TJ Maxx or Marshall's.

3. When buying a house for the first time, be willing to buy foreclosures and fix them up.

4. When buying a "permanent" (you plan on living there for 7 years or more) residence, always buy from a "distressed seller" (i.e., foreclosure or short sale) as you'll get 40% more house for the same price.

5. Go to community college for two years and transfer to a larger, "more prestigious" state school.

6. When a new iPhone or iPad comes out, buy the older version for less. The new versions seldom have noticeable improvements.

7. Buy your cars at an auction or from distressed sellers.

SECTION 4 § CHAPTER 2

DON'T WASTE $30K ON THE STARTER WEDDING ... OR GIVE $500K TO THE STARTER SPOUSE

Our society has convinced all young girls they need an extravagant, fairy-tale wedding. Worse, their baby boomer parents have pushed this to the extreme where the average wedding now costs over $15,000 and many people spend over $30,000. This is absurd. A wedding should be a small, private affair with family and close friends. If desired, a simple, inexpensive party (max. $5,000) can follow. Any gifts should be in cash to help with a large downpayment on a house. With the divorce rate exceeding 50%, don't waste the money.

And what is the biggest and most costly financial mistake you can make? Divorce. I speak from personal experience on this one. I had to give my ex-wife $500,000 out of the after-tax profits from the business I sold as part of the divorce. Think about it—what is the most common argument between married couples? Money. Getting married too young and not being financially secure is a huge mistake. As I look back, it was definitely my fault getting married too early – I certainly don't blame it on my ex-wife. It is also a lot easier to protect assets that you brought into the marriage with a prenup than assets you accumulated during a marriage. Michael Jordan got married shortly after entering the NBA when he was in his early twenties. His divorce reportedly cost him $160 million. Tiger Woods's divorce cost him at least

$100 million. As one of my buddies used to say, his wife made him a millionaire…but he had $3 million when he married her.

Another huge cost is raising children. Don't get me wrong—I wouldn't trade my kids for the world. Kids are great, but don't underestimate the costs. According to the U.S. Government, the cost to raise a child from birth to age eighteen for a family with a gross income of $75,000 is $249,180. This total includes housing, food, transportation, K-12 education, clothing, healthcare, and a few bucks thrown in for miscellaneous expenses. The monthly breakout is $1,164. With current costs increasing around 6% per year, you can count on that figure rising to $2,000 per month within ten years. But guess what? …That doesn't include post-high-school education costs, which will be a minimum of $20,000 and could be as high as $200,000 per child if you still follow the traditional route!

M$M Star Tips

Absolutely, Positively Do Not Get Married Until Age Thirty

There is no reason to get married before age thirty at the earliest. Most of us grow and change enormously in our twenties—getting out of school, the first job or two, perhaps a new business.

Your chance of a successful marriage will improve dramatically if you have some financial security and know yourself first.

SECTION 4 § CHAPTER 3

AVOID THE BIGGEST PONZI SCHEME OF ALL

I was involved in the financial planning industry for eleven years, first as an owner of a broker-dealer that had over four hundred financial planners and then as a top producer in the business. The financial business—and it is a huge business, from the wheeler-dealers on Wall Street to *all* the advisors dealing with individual investors—is a major scam. It's a sales and publicity game that provides a huge benefit to the firms and their sales reps, but very little, if any, benefit to the individual investor. The dysfunction of this system is a big reason for the huge income disparity in this country. So here's the question: when will Americans finally give up on the Wall Street shenanigans?

The Wall Street scams have been going on for decades. In the late 1980s, Wall Street hyped/sold the heck out of high yield/junk bonds, which then plummeted from 1990 to '91. Then adjustable-rate mortgage funds were all the rage in the early 1990s as a safe, higher-yielding option than a money market. By 1992, investors had lost over $20 billion in these funds. In the late 1990s, it was the endless hyping of the Internet stocks and funds and then their collapse (down over 80%) from 2000 to 2003. A more recent scam was auction rate securities. Here's the pitch I got from the local Merrill Lynch broker in late 2008. He actually stopped by my house uninvited (a.k.a. desperate): "Mike, are you looking for a little higher yield (approximately

2% higher) on your money market funds without taking any more risk? We have a super-safe fund that allows you to get higher returns without any risk to your principal. The only catch is that you can only get your money out every seven days. All you have to do is call me a couple days before you need your funds and then I can wire you your funds in a couple of days." Now, the older I get, the more suspicious I am of "great" deals. My red flag was the seven-day redemption—what the heck was that? The broker didn't know—said it was how the product worked (i.e., "trust me"). I told him to beat it, but I thought to myself, "I bet they are selling a ton of this junk, whatever it is." Turns out he was selling auction rate securities, though that term was never mentioned to me and I'm sure not to other investors. The big brokerage firms peddling this garbage stuck investors with over $50 billion in losses. Think how pissed you would be if you stuck $100,000 of your emergency funds in a supposedly "super-safe" investment and your trusty broker told you it was now gone!

Do we even need to talk about the subprime scam that the Wall Street wizards were putting over on all of us in the mid to late 2000s? Providing capital to fund mortgages to anyone who could breathe—who cares if they could repay the loan?—was a sound financial game plan, wasn't it? And the fact that the big investment banks were selling this garbage at the same time they were making huge bets that the entire housing market would all crumble wasn't a conflict of interest, was it? And now Wall Street is dominated by the rapid-fire "black box" trading platforms of the highly leveraged hedge funds that make trades by the millisecond. *The average blackbox traders, which account for up to 70% of the daily activity on Wall Street, hold stocks for an average of eleven seconds!* The stock market has become a place for short-term traders to gamble their money, not a long-term wealth-building platform for the average unsophisticated investor.

But diversification still works, doesn't it? It didn't work from 2007 to 2009, when almost every asset class went down big—

US stocks, emerging market stocks, gold, utilities, high yield, corporate bonds, etc. Diversification, when done properly, may get you to 7%–8% annually, but there will be a lot of downside risk. And what does the average stock market investor do when the markets get rough? Most of them panic and sell, thus reducing their returns further. The problem with "timing" the market is that you have to be right twice—when to get out and when to get back in. It's very difficult to do successfully over several years.

The fact that most of the country has been conned into putting all their retirement assets into this Ponzi scheme is truly frightening! Enough! No more! You need to avoid stockbrokers, financial planners, or financial advisors, etc.—anyone working to earn a commission or *fee* by selling you products and services related to the stock market that don't have an implicit guarantee (key distinction – see Money Skillz #4 below), such as mutual funds, stocks, managed accounts, etc. Did you know that a top producer at any investment firm in the country is the one who generates the most commissions and/or fees for the firm? How he/she performs for his/her clients is not even a small consideration. He/she has a *huge* conflict of interest—he/she needs to sell you something to put food on his/her table.

Don't think things have changed at all since the Great Recession of 2008–09. Greg Smith, a partner at one of the big Wall Street banks, put an op-ed in the *New York Times* in March 2012 saying how he was quitting the firm after twelve years because the firm's "environment now is as toxic and destructive as I've ever seen it." The op-ed describes how the firm is driven by how much money it makes off its client, not what's best for the client. Nothing has changed.

And here's a bigger secret—most financial salesman know as little as you do about successful investing. In order to be successful, they need to know how to sell, not how to invest. Who teaches them how to sell? The mutual fund companies pushing their overpriced products! Here's the one question you must ask any financial salesman: show me independently verifiable results that your moderate-risk clients—i.e., a mix of 60% stocks and 40% bonds—have returned an average of 8% or more per year after fees for the last ten years. Less than 5% will produce their numbers. Why? Because they don't track that. They only track their commissions!

A story here in Raleigh, where I live, caught my eye recently. The former CEO of a local Fortune 500 tech company was suing his "investment advisor" for losing $60 million of his money in improper investments, including some tied to horse racing and strip clubs. The "investment advisor" must have been incredibly slick, as the CEO's children referred to him as "Uncle Jim" (a well-known trick for advisors is to try to become your buddy). What on earth was the CEO doing giving $60 million to an "investment advisor?" Put the money in a simple bond program and generate $2 million plus of investable income each year, a lot of it tax-free. But here is another example of a guy who probably knew a lot about technology and very little about personal finance.

And how have the mutual funds done that your esteemed advisor chose? Well, let's see, the S&P 500 has averaged 4.7% over the last 15 years, and that is before tax. I know, CNBC never mentions any period prior to the market bottom of 2009, so its easy to forget that the long-term averages are subpar and are achieved with a huge amount of ups and downs, primarily due to the way the Federal Reserve has massively manipulated the money supply by keeping rates at zero for too long. Is it me, or does this current artificially inflated stock market bring a strong *deja vu* of the 2003–2008 market all over again, where the Fed artificially pumped up the stock market and then it crashed? What do you think will happen to the stock market after the Fed is done manipulating it again and short-term interest rates go back to the normal 3%–5% instead of 0.5%? It won't be pretty. In fact, two legendary investors—Bill Gross, manager of the world's largest and one of the most successful bonds funds, called Pimco Total Return, and Jeremy Grantham, manager of

$38 billion in funds—are outspoken about the fact that they believe the market will have a hard time producing 7% average annual returns over the next ten to fifteen years!

Let me make this very clear: the salesmen are (usually) not breaking any laws by selling you these products. They are all products and services that are approved by federal and state regulators. Remember, the financial salesmen are trying to achieve their number one goal —feed their family (goal number two is making the Benz payment). Shame on you for being financially illiterate and buying these worthless products and services. I was in the business for over ten years, and I have zero assets directly linked to the stock market—no stocks, no bonds, no individual retirement accounts (IRAs – self directed IRA's are great for real estate investing though). You can make a lot more money investing in M$M businesses and real estate than messing with nonsense.

Wall Street is a good place when it allows small businesses to raise money from institutional (i.e. very sophisticated) investors to grow their businesses. It was never designed for the average American to bank 100% of their retirement dreams on it. I do see some glimmers of hope though. My friend Kevin Myers recently left his high-pressured investment banking job and became a financial advisor at TIAA-CREF, probably the biggest financial services company you've never heard about. He is paid a fixed salary with no commission. He says the training and education are excellent and the focus is on "doing the right thing for the client in all situations." They only have low cost funds. Vanguard Funds has a similar program.

If you are going to invest in the stock market, you need to follow the study produced by Rick Ferri at Portfolio solutions. He did a study that showed investing in three Vanguard funds – 40% into Total Stock Market Index, 20% into Total International Stock Fund, and 40% in the Total Bond Market Index - beat more than 80% of all actively managed portfolios from 1997-2012. For most people, there is no need to consider any other strategy.

M$M Star Tips

YOU CAN'T AFFORD TO LOSE MONEY

The huge drops in the stock market from 2001 to 2003 and again from 2008 to 2009 gave a lot of smaller investors a huge wake-up call on the dangers of losing money. Most people have not saved enough to live a comfortable retirement, so big losses to their portfolios are crushing.

Look at the simple example below using $10,000:

	Return	Value
Year 1	8%	$10,800
Year 2	4%	$11,232
Year 3	9%	$12,242
Year 4	3%	$12,610
Year 5	-10%	$11,343
Year 6	?	

What rate of return do you need in year six just to get back to a 5% annualized return? The answer is 19%, which is really hard to get. The average investor can't afford to play the Ponzi scheme of the stock market because he/she can't afford losses!

SECTION 4 § CHAPTER 4

INVESTING SHOULD BE S-O-O-O-O EASY...

Here's my simple M$M strategy for managing the money you don't want to allocate to your M$M businesses:

Under Age Thirty Five – Focus on Liquidity: When you are under the age of thirty-five, I believe most of your money needs to go into cash and into investing in your own business and/or real estate. I really like the concept of opening a Roth IRA in an FDIC-insured-bank money market. With the Roth, all future profits are tax free, which is great with tax rates surely headed up one way or another. Also with a Roth, you can withdraw the principal amount at any time without penalty, so it works well for an emergency fund (remember—eighteen months of living expenses need to be in cash). You can also use your Roth to make real estate investments by setting up your account at a firm like Equity Trust (www.trustetc.com).

If you have a 401(k), I would only put in an amount that is equal to the employer match, because that is free money. I would put all other funds toward "owning" something—either an M$M business, an affordable housing investment, or your house.

You need to buy term life insurance during this stage only if you have a wife or family.

Age Thirty-Six to Age Sixty – Start a Pension Fund: Once you get established and hopefully on target to being an M$M, you should have some excess money and should diversify into more conservative investments.

Instead of rolling the dice on the Ponzi stock market, you need to think about stability. Where are you going to get stability in this day and age? Highly rated insurance companies. Two products I like from them:

1. A whole life insurance policy that is over funded. OK, I know all the financial gurus tell you to run from this product because of the costs involved, but they also tell you to load up on worthless mutual funds. As an M$M, I take risks in my business or real estate, not in anything else. I like the whole life policy (I use Northwestern Mutual) because it pays a steady 5%–7%, it covers a big chunk of my life insurance needs (which grow as you get more successful), and it provides great tax advantages. I overfund my policy (put in the most allowed by law) to maximize the cash accumulation. I can also turn this product into a monthly annuity payment in retirement. Pamela Yellen has done a great job illustrating this concept at www.bankonyourself.com—go there and get educated. This product is designed for people with larger life insurance needs and at least $500,000 in investable assets.

M$M Star Tips

THE NEW SOCIAL SECURITY PROVIDERS

People under fifty-five need to realize they will receive significantly less Social Security than their parents received. Thus, they need to find a new, safe, guaranteed retirement income source. The insurance companies and their salesmen are the providers of these new "pensions," which can provide steady streams of income in retirement and replace the Social Security payments.

2. An equity-indexed annuity or variable annuity with a guaranteed income rider (the only way I recommend having any stock market exposure) which guarantees your account value will go up every year. Again, the current financial pundits hate these products because of the heavy commissions involved and their complexity. But they do one important thing—*they never lose money!* In my opinion, they are designed to return 5%–7% without downside risk (remember, most market experts believe you will have a difficult time getting 7% in the market over the next decade). So what if the insurance broker gets paid? He/she is offering you peace of mind. I would only use these products if I didn't have large life insurance needs, and I would definitely go with the top-rated companies (see the M$M Toolbox at the end of the book for more companies).

AN AFFORDABLE RENTAL HOUSE IN AN IRA?

I am a big fan of cash flowing real estate, and a retirement asset I really like for IRA's is an affordable single-family rental house. I think affordable, single-family rental houses are one of the best, if not the best, investments available today. Both Donald Trump and Warren Buffet have recently said that they think single-family rental properties are the best investment for 2013. Most people don't know that you can use your IRA funds to purchase affordable rental houses. In most cases, I would recommend buying the homes for cash (usually in the $70K–$100K range) and aim for an 8%–12% return after management fees, expenses, and some vacancy factored in. Having an experienced "turnkey" property manager who buys the homes, rehabs them, leases them up, and then provides ongoing management is key.

You can also buy these properties outside of your IRA and use leverage, i.e., take out a loan on each home. For example, if you bought six homes for $80,000 each, you would only use about $150,000 of funds (figure $1,000 in closing costs each) if you put 30% down. If you use a fifteen-year mortgage, that $150,000 would grow to $450,000 in fifteen years, with the debt pay down alone about a 4.5% return. Plus, you should be getting 8%–12% on top of that in net cash flow, for a total return of 12.5%–16.5%! If you are lucky enough to get 2% appreciation, your $150,000 could turn into $1 million! The homes also provide a great hedge against inflation, which could comeback with the relentless money printing the Fed is doing. You can easily find and manage these houses yourself, though I would caution that being a part-time landlord is not easy.

As you hit age forty, you need to up your cash liquidity to two years' worth of living expenses. If you can't do it, it means your lifestyle needs to come down a notch.

Age Sixty Plus: A true M$M never retires, but if you want to slow down, my recommendation is to make sure you have assets that can produce cash flow when you need it, like the whole life insurance product, the guaranteed annuities, and affordable rental houses with no debt on them. Having products that allow you to turn on the cash flow with a simple maneuver when needed in retirement is huge. Always keep three to four years' worth of living expenses liquid in retirement.

SECTION 4 § CHAPTER 5

PAY OFF THE CRIB!

The big mantra during the bubble times of the early 2000s was that everyone had to own a home. Lenders were offering 100% financing and making loans to people who couldn't realistically pay those mortgages— forget maintaining the homes! People who never thought they'd be able to "afford" a home bought in—after all, if the bank thinks I can afford the house, I must be able to, right? The result is the catastrophe we now have—home prices down 30% nationally and probably going down 40%, tons of homes for sale, tons of vacant and foreclosed homes. And now the lenders are all crying at the losses in their real estate portfolios. I'll never forget the golf outing we had in our gated community in Orlando in June of 2005. Every person there was talking about how much equity he/she had in his/her home—like it was his/her own personal ATM. Homes that were bought for $250,000 were selling for $400,000 less than two years later. Everyone was caught up in it. I turned to my neighbor Paul and said, "If this isn't the top of the market, I don't know what is." My wife and I sold our house in Orlando in the fall of 2006 after living there less than three years and were thrilled to make $100K in profit, but our neighbors complained because we sold it too low! We got out at the right time, though. That house plunged over $100K in value and still isn't worth what we sold it for eight years later even with the housing recovery! I firmly believe the 2003-2007 housing bubble was a once-in-a-lifetime experience.

My opinion is that homeownership is way overrated. In fact, I have read two recent articles that state that investing in a house to live in is never as good a financial move as renting! I totally agree. The carrying costs associated with a house are always underestimated. The only reason to buy a house to live in (not to be confused with a house you own for rental purposes) is for lifestyle choices, i.e., somewhere comfortable to live for your family. Below are the new rules (if you're over forty, you'll recognize these are the old rules) for homeownership:

1. **Buy a house to reside in only if you are going to live in it for seven or more years**. The cost of real estate commissions, closing costs, maintenance, etc., will not make it profitable. There are thousands of nice homes for rent at a reasonable price. My buddy Gary in Wisconsin (not a boom-and-bust market) sold his home in early 2008 after living in it for eight years. After real estate commissions, landscaping, and other minor improvements, he ended up losing $10,000.

2. **Buy an affordable house and pay it off in fifteen to twenty years**. Affordability will be determined by the cost of the fifteen or twenty-year mortgage. And forget the Wall Street "rule" that says you should never pay off your mortgage because you can earn a higher rate of return in the stock market. That was further Wall Street garbage sold to create more fees and commissions.

3. **Buy a house only with a minimum 20% down payment**. You need to be able to afford the house. Rent until you can afford it. Don't stretch to buy something—you will regret it; there are always unplanned expenses, and job security just isn't there anymore. The costs of owning a house—i.e., new furniture, regular maintenance, capital improvements (new roof)—are far more than you think. I would also recommend you put money aside each month toward future maintenance and repair expenses. Learn the life expectancies of your roof, plumbing, carpet, appliances, etc., and budget accordingly.

4. Never buy a condo. The homeowner fees and assessments for capital improvements on condos will kill you. Rent the condo unless you are going to stay in it for a minimum of ten years. Even at ten years, your chances of making money are very slim. My buddy Jim has a condo he bought in Orlando in 1992 for $95,000. Thirteen years later he tried to sell the condo for $125,000. It was for sale for almost two years and he didn't get any offers. None. He has it rented now, which covers his payment because his basis is so low in it, but his condo fees have quadrupled since he's owned it to $430 a month!

5. Never buy a second home. This is a huge fallacy of the bubble times of the 2000s. You are much better off renting a vacation home, even if it is for six months during the winter. The appreciation in these homes has vanished overnight and will not be coming back for a long time. And if you're on the beach, the insurance costs will be sky high. There are a ton of vacation homes for rent at reasonable prices.

For those of you stuck in corporate America, I recommend that you stop contributing to your 401(k) above the company match (i.e., if the match is 5%, only contribute 5%) and instead use that money to pay off the crib! What is the advantage of paying off your house? If you have a $250,000 mortgage at 6% interest and pay it off in thirty years, it will cost you $289,595 in interest. If you pay it off in twenty years, it will cost you $179,858 in interest, a savings of $109,737, plus you will get an additional $2,000-plus more per month in cash during years 21-30. More important, you get huge peace of mind! The rate of return you will get by paying off your house early is close to 5% and it's guaranteed!

M$M Star Tips

THIS TAX BREAK IS TOAST

I know you have constantly heard that the tax break you get with the mortgage interest deduction makes it worthwhile to keep a high mortgage and invest the rest in the stock market. I strongly disagree. Even if you factor in the mortgage interest savings, your net return by paying your home off early is in the range of 5%.

And that return is guaranteed! Experts believe investors will struggle to make a 7% return in the market over the next ten to fifteen years. The risk for an extra 2% is not worth it. Furthermore, it is very likely that the home mortgage interest deduction will get wiped out in the next couple of years as a compromise to reduce the deficit.

Bottom line: *Main $treet Millionaires* pay off their cribs by age fifty!

SECTION 4 § CHAPTER 6

DON'T EVER GIVE YOUR MONEY TO... AN AFRICAN BUSINESSMAN... A CONDO DEVELOPER... A THUMPER... YOUR UNCLE ...OR A TIME-SHARE SALESMAN

It amazes me how otherwise smart people fall for investment scams that promise to give them a 10% return *per month*, or to double their money in twelvemonths, etc. Think of all the scams that have come to light in the last couple years—Bernie Madoff (never had a losing year), Alan Stanford (guaranteed 12% per year returns from offshore CDs), and on and on. It seems like we read about one or two every month now.

I'll never forget sitting down in late 2008 to talk with a mid-level money manager from Louisiana about an investment he had made into a mobile home community Ponzi scheme. I was trying to buy one of the communities tied up in the scam and was trying to find out what had happened with the investors. After we discussed the catastrophe of the mobile home scam (seven investors lost over $3 million on this one community, and over two hundred investors lost almost $75 million total amongst twenty or so communities), this supposedly astute money manager started telling me about an investment that guaranteed a minimum return of 12% that he had with a big money manager in the Caribbean. He claimed that the more volatile the stock market was, the better the investment would perform.

What? I told him I didn't think that was possible, but he told me it was legit. Turns out it was an investment with an organization run by Alan Stanford, the guy who just got convicted for running a massive Ponzi scheme. The guy I was talking to ended up losing another $3 million of his investors' money (I'm sure he didn't have any of his own money invested).

Another age-old adage to remember: *"If it sounds too good to be true, it is!"* If the stock market has returned an average of 7%–8% per year for the last thirty years and a five-year CD is returning 1% per year, how the hell can someone generate 10% per month? Don't believe it. It doesn't happen. Here are some other tips:

- If any investment person starts a meeting with a prayer or starts talking about God, run...fast. I have seen several people mix religion and investments and the results are never pretty. Guess how the mobile home park Ponzi scheme operator discussed above signed all his letters? You guessed it—"God Bless." He also started every meeting with a prayer—which I guess all the investors badly needed because they were about to lose everything.

- Never make a check out to a financial advisor or to his company—you never know where it's going. Only make the check out to the insurance company or your IRA custodian.

- If your uncle hits you up for the "greatest business or investment opportunity ever," run...fast. Make sure you have your hand on your wallet when you are dashing away.

- If you receive an unsolicited e-mail from a Nigerian businessman or English money tycoon promising you a phat return if you will just wire him $10K upfront, please delete it! Quickly.

- Never, ever chase a "hot" stock tip from a friend or a relative—just stay away from the stock market entirely and you'll save yourself a lot of grief.

- If you get the "free vacation" flyer in the mail, toss it immediately into the recycle bin. The "free" involves sitting through a brutal, high- pressure sales situation to buy a timeshare condo that will depreciate in value by at least 50% the day you buy it! Never, ever buy a timeshare—the fees will kill you. You can always stay at a hotel or rent a condo much cheaper.

- Never chase the latest investment scam. I know several people who got hammered in the condo craze in Florida in the 2000s. Remember that scam? If you were "lucky," the condo developer would let you in on "preconstruction prices" because they were supposedly going to double by the time they were completed eighteen months later. Didn't quite work out that way.

I definitely throw real estate developers into this mix because they are the most pie-eyed optimists ever. They have no cash flow to back up their projects, only far-off promises. The preconstruction purchase, the condo conversion, the condo-hotel—all ridiculous scams. Here's the question you need to ask yourself with regard to real estate developers: if the development has such a great return, how come they need your money? Do you think they just want to spread the wealth? Hell no. They want to use *your money* so if they lose, *they aren't losing their own money.* And if they win, they reap a bunch of fees and share in the upside profits without risking their own money. Hedge funds operate the same way.

Another tip to avoid some grief is: never loan money to any friends or family members unless you have no expectations you will get the money back. I am going through a situation where a buddy got way overextended and I loaned him $10K. He gave me this concocted plan for how he would pay all the money back quickly. Two weeks after I loaned him the $10K, he called asking for another $10K. I said no. I now get $100 payments each month. It will probably take eight years to get my principal back if I'm lucky.

Stick to the simple investment system of controlling your own financial destiny by buying cash-flowing M$M businesses and real estate!

SECTION 4 § CHAPTER 7

BE FINANCIALLY SECURE BY AGE FIFTY

One of the key goals of being a *Main Street Millionaire* is that you need to be financially secure by the age of fifty. Why age fifty? First, if you are in corporate America, they will put a target on your back at the age of fifty because they don't want to pay your health insurance costs. Besides, it's cheaper for them to bring in a thirty-year-old, who is probably much more technologically savvy, for half what they pay you. And once you get canned from your decent-paying job after the age of fifty, good luck trying to land another job with even 60% of your prior pay.

My neighbor got laid off from a mid-level management position at Caterpillar at the age of fifty-three. He was out of work for almost six months. He was fortunate to get rehired at Caterpillar, but he was forced to commute to Peoria, Illinois (from North Carolina), and the cost of transportation is on him. Even worse, he's making less money than he was before.

Second, if you can reach financial freedom by age fifty, you can hopefully have a lot of years to pursue your passions. Life is so much better when you are doing something you really love to do, rather than being forced to punch the corporate clock until you are seventy.

What does "financially free" mean? It all depends on your lifestyle, but the following are *minimum* components for a *Main*

Street Millionaire:

- House paid off or sold—$2,500 per month maximum in home payments (mortgage, taxes, insurance, upkeep) or rent.

- A minimum of two years' living expenses in cash, moving toward the goal of three years' worth of cash.

- At least one cash flow asset that produces $4,000 per month in net income. If it's real estate, the asset needs to have less than 50% leverage on it using a conservative valuation.

Being financially free at age fifty doesn't mean you have to stop working; it just means you can put your corporate job on probation—i.e., if they ever piss you off, you're gone. Everyone in Corporate America is still on edge waiting for the next economic downturn to cause another round of layoffs. Financial freedom means not having to worry about whether your boss will give you the ax or having to work a minimum wage job until you are eighty-five because you haven't saved enough.

If you do get laid off before you've reached financial freedom, don't panic. Step back and take a good look at where you are and where you'd like to be. There are some great resources out there—but you need to take the right steps.

Here's what you don't want to do in your fifties and sixties. David Lundin, was an employee for twenty-six years at General Motors who got ousted in the 2008–09 turmoil at GM. Lundin had access to supposedly "professional" outplacement services, and they advised him to go back school, which was mistake number one. So he spent about $50K and got a degree in psychotherapy. Now he was all set, except he couldn't find a job in his new field that would even pay him $30K because every business in America is petrified to hire anyone over the age of fifty-five because of health care costs. So Mr. Lundin was advised to make mistake number two: invest in a franchise (see Biz Skillz #5 in Section 4 on the franchise scam). He invested over $100,000 in some scam franchise and he hasn't made a dime of profit yet (like most franchises)! Not only was he pushed out of his corporate job sooner than expected, he ended up making two very common and costly mistakes made by American workers in their fifties and sixties.

What should he have done? First, he should have closely studied the M$M businesses I listed above. Second, he should have worked in one or more of the businesses for at least a year or two (getting paid all the while) before he even thought about venturing out on his own. Moreover, being in the Detroit area, he could have bought five quality, affordable rental houses for the $100,000 he spent on the scam franchise, turned them over to a qualified property management company, and he would be sitting pretty right now.

M$M MONEY SKILLZ RECAP

- "Spend less than you make." Wow—what a concept.

- Live in the basement as long as you can. You can save $$, and Mom may still do your laundry.

- Wait to get married until age thirty, and make the wedding small. Use the money to buy cash-flowing assets instead.

- Don't give $500K to the starter spouse. Divorce is the biggest financial mistake you can make.

- The stock market is a big Ponzi scheme. You've got better options.

- Pay off the crib as fast as possible.

- If it sounds too good to be true...it is.

- You've gotta be financially secure by age fifty—especially if you work in Corporate America.

SECTION 5

M$M BIZ SKILLZ

Formal education will make you a living.
Self-education will make you a fortune.
~ Jim Rohn

I truly believe that my kids and the rest of the younger generation face a very difficult future and will be *the first generation in American history to be worse off than their parents!* Two depressing stats:

- The unemployment rate for sixteen to twenty-four-year-olds is still over 14%, and almost one million sixteen to twenty-four-year-olds are considered NEET—Not in Education, Employment, or Training.

- The average twenty-five-year-old worker can expect to pay $175,000 more in Social Security taxes over his/her lifetime than he/she will receive back, if he/she receives any back at all. Nothing like having Grandma and Grandpa garnish 10% of your wages every week for the next thirty-five years!

If I were in my late teens or early twenties, I would be pissed that my future opportunities are significantly less than any other generation in the last seventy-five years. The fifty-five-plus generation has bankrupted the country and has no interest in having their taxes raised or taking one penny less in Social Security and Medicare than they are currently entitled to receive. The wealth gap between the average household headed by a sixty-five-year-old and that of the household headed by the average thirty-five-year-old is the widest in U.S. history and has increased by five times since 2005! But I know: it's a lot easier to spend the day playing World of Warcraft than to face reality.

I am a big believer that entrepreneurship is a far better path than Corporate America today. The Great Recession shed over six million jobs, and millions more people are underemployed or have simply quit trying to find a job. I don't know anyone who likes his/her corporate job, and it doesn't matter the industry—technology, retail, real estate, law, etc. The demands corporations put on their (remaining) employees are huge—a minimum of sixty hours per week, nonstop communication via the smartphone, employees afraid to take vacation, and enormous pressure to "toe the company line." Job satisfaction in Corporate America is at an all -time low. Is this really how you want to live your life?

There are a few satisfying "corporate" jobs out there, but don't think they will allow you to escape the corporate misery. In fact, Reid Hoffman, founder of LinkedIn and an early investor in Zynga and Facebook, says in his book, *The Start-up of You*, that "the old paradigm of climb up a stable career ladder is dead." You should approach your career the same way an entrepreneur approaches a business." Many businesses in Silicon Valley now assess their employees *every quarter* to see if they are still needed because things are changing so fast. The high-tech corporate world has great opportunities, but it's also a cutthroat, dog-eat-dog environment.

I saw a great quote from Susan Ascher, a recruiter from New Jersey, explaining the new deal with Corporate America: "The social contract between companies and workers was first broken with the recession of the early 1990s, and it has only gotten worse. *A so-called permanent corporate job is really a temporary job disguised with benefits.*"

Face it, Corporate America is a huge buzz kill. My neighbor told me his company's philosophy is: "If you disagree with a policy, don't complain, just find something to like about it." There is no dissension allowed. And we all know there are no guarantees in Corporate America anymore. Do you really want to go to school for twelve years, then spend a fortune on a degree, to end up in corporate slavery? I've been there and, trust me, it sucks! But the corporate trap is easy to fall into: You start making a decent salary, you get married, you buy a house, you have two kids, and boom—you're trapped! Your mortgage and kids are expensive. You need the corporate job to keep your standard of living. Beware! This scenario afflicts a vast majority of corporate droids.

So you need to ask yourself the big question: *Is there really more risk today in owning your own cash-flowing business than being a stooge in Corporate America?* I say *no*—the risk is the same now! Furthermore, Corporate America is going to force you into being an entrepreneur when you get over the age of fifty anyway, so you might as well start early on your path to becoming a *Main Street Millionaire.*

Many people describe owning your own business as a roller coaster because it tends to have higher highs and lower lows than a corporate job. But I would argue neither Corporate America nor entrepreneurship *is going to be a smooth ride* anymore, so either way, you will have to expect obstacles and learn how to get past them. But here's the key —for the vast majority of people, entrepreneurship gives you a far better shot at achieving financial freedom than Corporate America! Once I got my first taste of truly owning a business (where I put up my own money and actually owned the business — i.e., I had "skin in the game"), I never looked back and feel very blessed to have had the opportunity.

If you're going to be an M$M, you've got to learn to accept risk, which is easier said than done for most people. Mark Cuban, the billionaire owner of the Dallas Mavericks, recently tackled the topic of "How to Get Rich" on his blog. His answers were quite refreshing. First, there are no shortcuts.

Second, live on mac and cheese—no going out, no credit cards, etc. (see "M$M Money Skillz"). Third, find a job relating to a business that you are passionate about, even if it means starting at the bottom. Spend every day, including weekends, learning the business. This may take years or even decades. Finally, wait for times of uncertainty or change in the industry and jump on the opportunities that arise. This is the key. You must be prepared to take action!

Now it seems like almost everyone I know is venturing into the entrepreneurship world:

- My friend Punkage Gupta is an accomplished ear, nose, and throat (ENT) doctor. He bucked the current trend for doctors and told the big health maintenance organization/ hospital to take a hike after ten years and started his own practice. After an up-and-down initial year, he is now making almost as much money as he was being a "corporate" doctor, as he puts it, and has a lot more control over his destiny, including the ability to explore other investment opportunities related to his practice which he never had time to do in "corporate" medicine.

- My buddy from high school, Steve Van Remortel, got booted out of his vice president of corporate sales job when the company he worked for got sold over twelve years ago. He vowed that he would never go through that BS again, so he started his own consulting business from scratch. After several lean years starting out, he now clears $250K each year with ease.

- My buddy and one of my investors, Jim Balletta, recently went part time at his law firm at age fifty-two (he was a partner for ten-plus years) because he hated the grind. He scaled down his personal expenses a touch, and his "passive" income now exceeds $100K per year, in

addition to having over $1 million in other assets (an
M$M requirement for being financially free at age fifty!).
His advice for young attorneys: get out while you can!
The law business is a horrible grind.

I've seen example after example where people just get fed up with working for others and getting nowhere. From my hairstylist, Franca, who is just starting her own shop, to my buddy Canelle, who started a mobile car wash/pressure wash biz, these folks all know that the only way to get financially-free in America today is to *own cash-flow-producing assets*, such as a business or real estate. Like me, they have all worked in Corporate America and gotten fed up with the bull.

SECTION 5 § CHAPTER 1

COLLEGE IS A HUGE WASTE OF MONEY

One area that has gotten totally out of hand is the cost and *value* of a college education. High school guidance counselors and parents in America push their kids to a four or five-year degree because it's "prestigious" to talk about their "college grad." But not every kid excels at or enjoys academics, and, despite what others may tell you, there's nothing wrong with that! Did you know that according to a Department of Education survey, 30% of college students drop out in the first year, and almost 50% never graduate?

I believe at least 50% of the high school graduates who head to college each year are wasting their money, and that percentage is only going to go up as our economy/way of life careens toward third-world status. What a waste of time, and then there's the money. A recent study by two New York University professors, Richard Arum and Joseph Roksa, found that a large number of students were making their way through college with minimal exposure to rigorous coursework, only a modest investment of effort, and little or no meaningful improvement in skills like writing or reasoning.

Their study showed the average student spent an average of twelve to thirteen hours per week studying. I totally agree with their findings - most of my friends and I treated college as a joke. It was a place to party three or four nights a week.

But here's the problem: *College tuition is now four hundred times more expensive than it was thirty years ago!* **Four hundred times!** Public college costs in North Carolina have risen over 45% in the last four years alone! And what are the two biggest factors contributing to the soaring price of tuition? A ridiculous amount spent on new buildings and the steep rise in college presidents' and senior administrators' salaries. In fact, over thirty-six college presidents now make over $1 million a year. Don't even get me started about the cost of a private college! And after you shell out all this money and end up in debt up to your eyeballs, if you don't have a marketable skill, there's a good chance you'll end up unemployed or underemployed. Is the benefit worth the cost? Do multimillion-dollar new buildings and overpaid college presidents and administrators really help the students? *The piece of paper, a.k.a. the college degree, is way overpriced if it doesn't translate into a bankable skill that directly translates into earning money.*

Colleges constantly bombard you with the fact that college grads make a lot more coin than those without a degree. That may have been true for people who went to college in the 1960's through the 1980's, but not anymore. The great college myth needs to be debunked. Here are the hypothetical numbers for our new friends, Will and Ned:

Will and Ned each go on an excellent adventure. Both saved up $20,000 for college. However, Will decides to skip college and start working at age eighteen. He puts his $20,000 into an affordable rental house investment netting only 7% per year. He makes the average yearly pay for a high school graduate with no college, approximately $18,750 per year ($9 per hour) and peaks at around $15 per hour, or $31,200 per year at age sixty. Each month he adds $100 of his after-tax income into paying off his rental home mortgage. He is able to live in his parents' basement, so he pays no room and board for the next five years.

Ned has a more typical college experience. He goes to a big public university. He switches majors once, so he ends up graduating in five years. His total cost for the five years, including room, board, and tuition, is $65,375. Because Ned has only saved $20,000, he is forced to take a loan out for $45,375 at 5% over twelve years, which equals $419 per month. Ned will start out with an average pay for recent graduates of $26,000 per year and peak near $60,000. He can't put any money into investments until he pays off his student loan in twelve years. From age thirty-five until age sixty, Ned puts the money he had paid on the student loans ($419 per month) into a mutual fund earning (hopefully) 7% to try and catch up.

Who has more money at age sixty? Ned ends up with $339,420, but Will has $679,469! Is college worth it? Try running these numbers for law school, where the average debt is another $37,000 on top of the $45,375 that Will had to take out. The lawyer would have to invest $1,000 per month after taxes in a 7% account just to match Will's investment numbers.

I wouldn't even consider sending my kids to a private college. I went to a private college and it was a huge waste of money. But OK, I hear the whining already—"but my child will be missing out on the college 'experience' and 'networking.' " What is that college experience really? Binge drinking, laziness, about twenty-five hours a week spent on class and studies, and a couple of years to "grow up"? You could get by with that in the old days, but not anymore. The world has changed drastically in the last few years. The job market is now global in nature and thus way more competitive and money is much tighter. And as for "networking," most people I know after being out of college for ten years only communicate with college friends occasionally on Facebook. "Networking" is done in your business and your profession after college.

And please do not waste any money on these *for-profit* adult education/online programs offered by the numerous big players in that industry. I call that industry adult porn because that's what most of it is. These programs are way overpriced and sock low-income students with huge amounts of loans they can never pay back. Their "admissions" people are really just commissioned salespeople trying to ring up loans on any student who breathes. The fact that these institutions have been allowed to get almost 90% of their revenue from the federal government and operate without any regulations is a travesty.

Finally, I would avoid getting an advanced degree unless you are really committed to climbing the corporate ladder. For the $75,000–$125,000 it will cost you, I don't think a master's degree in business or a law degree is close to being worth it. The law degree is especially tricky now, as there are lots of unemployed lawyers and underemployed lawyers. An example of the lack of legal jobs comes from my brother-in-law, who is the president of a small law firm in Minneapolis. They have the contract for Legal Shield (formerly Pre-Paid Legal), which is a multilevel marketing business focused on providing affordable legal services to the masses. He is required to have ten to fifteen lawyers on staff just answering the phones. He pays these people around $15 per hour. When he runs an ad for this position, he gets flooded with resumes.

A recent New York Times article on the dismal prospects of the legal profession quoted Michael Wallerstein, a recent law school graduate who has $250K in student loan debt and no job. He said he was pleased with his education because he felt people now looked up to him because he was a "lawyer." What? Please! Prestige means nothing now except to your out-of-touch parents. Nobody cares if you are a lawyer or a doctor or a pawn shop owner. Before you even consider going to law school, read veteran lawyer Michael Trotter's new book Declining Prospects about the dismal state of the legal profession.

What's the best deal available in education today? Community college. A report recently released by the National Skills Coalition showed that 51% of all jobs in the southern states of the United States fell into the "middle skills" category—those that require more training than high school but not a traditional four-year degree. There are lots of jobs available to people with these skills—which they can get from the local community college! It's also the least expensive path to a four or five-year degree if you do your first two years at community college and live at home. You take the same classes as the four and five-year schools at 25% of the cost!

M$M Star Tips

Community College is the Way

According to a recent report by the Center for Education and the Workforce at Georgetown University, the number of jobs that will require a two-year degree will exceed the available applicants by over three million by 2018. Below is an example of jobs that only require a two-year degree and pay reasonably well:

Job	Average Salary
1. Computer/Tech Specialist	$59,480
2. Nuclear Technician	$59,200
3. Dental Hygienist	$58,350
4. Radiation Therapist	$57,700
5. Nuclear Medicine Tech	$55,840
6. Fashion Designer	$55,840
7. Aerospace Engineer Tech	$52,500
8. Medical Sonographer	$52,490
9. Registered Nurse	$52,330
10. Engineering Tech	$49,440

SECTION 5 § CHAPTER 2

M$Ms GOOGLE
THEIR EDUCATION

Sean Parker, an early investor in Facebook and other tech ventures and a college dropout, had a great quote when he was featured in the 2014 Forbes 400 (he has a net worth of a cool $2 billion). He said you should "skip college and Google your education. When these incredible tools of knowledge and learning are available to the whole world over the Internet, formal education becomes less and less important." I love it! In fact, sixty-three members of the Forbes 400 in 2014 never went to college.

I had my first real exposure to entrepreneurship when I bought into my first business—the financial broker-dealer—at age thirty-one. I had to make up for this lack of education by doing my own self-study over many years and making a lot of stupid mistakes to learn what I needed to know. Why was that? I never had any classes on personal finance, the basics of running a business, or entrepreneurship in high school, college, or law school. Not one. And worse, the Internet was in its infancy and I didn't have access to the vast knowledge available today. I can't stress strongly enough the importance of having a solid understanding of personal finance and entrepreneurship at a young age. It is essential to becoming an M$M, yet a vast majority of high schools and colleges don't require any study of the topic.

What is the new trend for elite athletes, musicians, dancers, actors, etc.? Start early and focus on one passion by the time you are fourteen. Why should expertise in personal finance or entrepreneurship be any different?

Parents need to make it a priority to get their kids educated on personal finance and entrepreneurship before they leave the house for college or start their first job. All the big entrepreneurs of our age—Bill Gates, Michael Dell, Donald Trump, Mark Cuban, Mark Zuckerberg, and others—were all encouraged by their parents to take risks and start businesses at a young age with very little capital. Now these guys are all billionaires. Go to juniorbiz.com and take a look at the top twenty-five junior entrepreneurs— it's impressive what they are doing.

So, your next question has to be—what if I am thirty-five, or forty-five, or fifty-five, and I don't have a clue about personal finance or entrepreneurship? Am I screwed? Absolutely not. It's never too late to start. With the current state of the economy and Corporate America's trend of pushing people over fifty out the door, you will probably be forced into entrepreneurship and face critical decisions regarding your own finances sooner than you think.

Let's be clear—I am a big proponent of education, but only if it is laser focused to one's strengths, produces a bankable skill, and is extremely cost effective. I just don't think most colleges provide these attributes to their students. How many times have you run into people like me who own businesses or are in career fields that have nothing to do with their college major? I would say 75% of the people I know are like this, yet everyone says you have to go to college to be successful. I don't think that is true anymore. Success in school, whether high school or college, involves toeing the line, not taking risks, and not making mistakes, the exact opposite skills required for success in any business venture today.

Peter Thiel, one of the founders of PayPal and the first outside board member of Facebook, is paying twenty people $100K each to pursue their entrepreneurial passions based on their business plan and one other criterion—they have to quit college to be eligible! One of the recipients of the $100,000 is Dale Stephens, who has started a business called uncollege.org that teaches kids to learn on their own without college.

Here are other examples, besides the numerous tech examples of Bill Gates, Steve Jobs, Mark Zuckerberg, Larry Ellison, etc., who have made it big without college:

1. My college roommate's father, Ralph Vennetti, Sr., flunked out of three colleges (never made it past a semester at any of them). He started working in sales and ended up owning two manufacturing businesses worth $15 million plus.

2. Brian Scudamore, the founder of 1-800-GOT-JUNK, started his business in 1989 with $700 and a pickup truck. He quit college halfway through to focus on his business. The firm now does over $75 million in sales all over the world.

3. Richard Branson, founder of the Virgin brand, quit school at age sixteen. He is now a billionaire.

4. Ralph Lauren was selling ties in high school but was determined to make it big in fashion. He dropped out of college in his second year and is now worth hundreds of millions.

5. John Paul Dejoria started Paul Mitchell Systems by selling shampoo door-to-door while living in his car. He is now worth $4 billion.

6. Phil Ruffin owns Treasure Island Casinos and has a net worth of $2.4 billion. His advice to young people: "Quit your job. Don't work for anyone else. You'll never make any money working for someone else."

7. Ted Turner, the founder of CNN, TNT, TBS, etc., got expelled from Brown University on his way to becoming a billionaire. His motto: "Start earlier and stay later than anyone else. You have to outwork the competition."

If you don't go to college, you will have a hard time succeeding in Corporate America, but that may be the best thing that ever happens to you. I firmly believe that if you get a baseline education in sales and personal finance/accounting and then use those skillz to buy M$M businesses and/or affordable housing investments, you will achieve far greater wealth and happiness than going to a four/five-year college will ever provide you.

As a side note, the continued soaring cost of a college education and the limited return that a degree provides opens up a huge opportunity for the entrepreneur who can provide an affordable, value-added practical education over the Internet. Companies like *Coursera* and *Learning Counts* are leading the way. Universities like Stanford, MIT, and Harvard are finally realizing their current model is toast over the long-term and are now providing low cost online classes by their best professors. The ability to provide low cost education to the masses is a huge opportunity. Another leader in the field is Salman Khan who started the Kahn Academy in 2006 by posting math lessons on YouTube. He now has over three thousand videos online and has raised millions from investors, primarily the Gates Foundation, to bring a quality education to the masses for very low cost.

M$M Star Tips

Top $100K-Plus Careers That Don't Require a College Degree

M$M Careers:

1. Affordable housing owner or regional manager
2. Pawn shop owner or manager of a larger store
3. Fast-food franchise owner or regional manager
4. Dollar store/rent-a-center owner or regional manager
5. Senior housing owner or regional manager
6. Insurance/pension salesman
7. Commercial real estate broker
8. Motivational coach/infopreneur

Others: (Require a two-year degree and five-plus years' experience)

1. Logistics manager
2. Air traffic controller
3. Construction superintendent
4. Radiation therapist
5. Mining site manager
6. Oil rig manager
7. Casino gaming manager
8. Director of security

SECTION 5 § CHAPTER 3

THE M$M FUNDAMENTALS OF ENTREPRENEURSHIP

The C-A-S-H-F-L-O-W mantra discussed in "M$M Money Skillz" also applies to "M$M Biz Skillz." Trust me—cash flow will carry you through the bad times. If you have a lot of positive cash flow, you can ride out the times when the value of your business fluctuates. You don't want to be in a position where there is no cash coming in and the value of the business or piece of real estate is dropping—that spells trouble. When I was in Florida in the mid-2000s, all the commercial real estate brokers kept approaching me and telling me that I was stupid for not converting my class B/C (i.e., affordable housing) apartment complexes to condos because I could make a ton of money.

Everything looked good on paper, but after analyzing the numbers closely, I realized that the profit came in selling the last 20% of the units. I kept asking them the question, "What if the units don't sell?" Of course they scoffed at me and told me they all would sell because "everybody gets a loan." I decided to stick to my boring old cash flow model, and guess what? Around 99.9% of the condo converters were forced into personal bankruptcy, and I sold our "boring" cash flow apartments for a lot more than they were worth. I guess I wasn't so stupid after all.

C – Cash flow businesses only. Only buy businesses or affordable housing properties that show a positive cash flow in the first month you own them. Buying anything that doesn't produce cash flow in one month is called speculation. *Main Street Millionaires* don't speculate.

A – Action is everything. I am a big reader and firmly believe in thoroughly preparing for any deal, project, etc. But I have also learned, with experience, that in every deal there are going to be issues that come up after the close; no deal is perfect. You have to prepare the best you can and then take a calculated risk.

S – Stalkers wanted. Before you get started, find a mentor in your particular business and do whatever you can to learn from him/her. When I was at the bank doing an internship after my second year of law school, I called up the CEO and told him who I was and that I would love to buy him lunch if he could tell me about his business experiences. He said he'd love to. People love to talk about themselves. Find someone that thinks like you and that you get along with, as mentorship needs to be a fun experience. And don't be afraid to switch mentors—many times the first person isn't the best fit.

H – Harvard is irrelevant. An Ivy League education is definitely not worth the cost in the entrepreneurship world. No one cares or even asks where you went to school. If you feel like you need to have the "piece of paper," your goal needs to be to get it with the least amount of cost possible, like going to community college for your first two years.

F – Failure is temporary. You are going to fail—count on it if you become an entrepreneur. What matters is how you respond to the failure. It's normal to want to quit. Are you going to walk away, or will you learn from your failure and move on? It didn't work—no biggie. I have had multiple personal and business failures, but I didn't quit, though it crossed my mind numerous times. Research Abe Lincoln, Colonel Sanders, etc.—I guarantee their list of failures is way longer than yours or mine.

L – Love what you do. Mort Zuckerman, the legendary real estate tycoon and owner/publisher of *US News & World Report*, said the best advice he ever got was from one of his professors at the Harvard Business School who told him that his success would come from doing something he loved. He was practicing law at the time, but he really loved the real estate business and journalism. So he quit his law practice and gave himself three years to make it in the real estate business. The result was spectacular, as he is one of the richest men in the country. Another great book you need to read is: *Do What You Love, the Money Will Follow*, by Marsha Sinetar; it had a big impact on my early life, as I was trying to be something I wasn't.

O – Own something. You make money in America by owning something, whether it be a cash flowing business or real estate investment or a highly specific and advanced skill, such as computer science, athletics, music, brain surgery, etc. Trading time for money, which is what most people in America are forced to do (think cashier, laborer, CPA, lawyer) is an endless grind. You have to work more hours for more money. Passive income is the key to financial freedom.

W – Whatever it takes. When you first enter the biz world, you have to be prepared to do whatever it takes (obviously with ethics and within legal limits) to get the job done. This is called the "bootstrap" stage. You will have to work a ton of hours (this is true in corporate America, too) and be prepared to do the lowly tasks, like bookkeeping, cleaning the store, etc. It's a lot easier to do the menial tasks when your money and livelihood are on the line. And I firmly believe that being in the trenches helps you build a much better business, because you understand all aspects of it.

MORE M$M ENTREPRENEURSHIP RULES TO CONSIDER

Below are some more M$M entrepreneurship fundamentals:

Never invest in something you don't understand or have prior experience in.

I've lost money on three businesses in my life, all of which I bought having no experience in the business prior to investing: my first venture into financial planning (totally naïve on the business); a small lawn care business we bought in Florida (you have to be the operator in that business unless you have large economies of scale); and a haircut franchise area developer (business seemed cool, but the numbers were terrible).

I've always made money on the other businesses I have owned because I understood them when I got in them: the broker-dealer (I ran the business for four-plus years before buying it); the financial planning practice (I spent seven years in the broker-dealer business learning how good practices were run); the apartments (we started small); the mobile home parks (learned a ton from the apartment business); and the property management business (we started it after having managed our own properties).

I highly recommend that anyone buying investment real estate or a business work in the business or apartment complex for a minimum of six months (and preferably one to two years) prior to purchase. If you're going to invest in something you don't understand and have no experience with, make sure it's a small investment.

You make your money at the purchase.

The best investments to buy, especially with a business or real estate, are the ones that still have a little positive cash flow but are underperforming due to mismanagement, the owner's lack of capital, etc. Always look for sellers who are motivated to sell—divorce, cash needs, etc. This is where experience in a particular business or real estate field is very important. You make your money at the purchase with these types of investments because your upside comes from getting the business or property to a normal, stabilized level. For example, I just placed an offer to purchase an apartment property that I sold in 2006 for $4.3 million. The price we offered—$320,000! It is completely vacant and owned by a bank that is desperate to get rid of it. I know we can get it to positive cash flow within ninety days because of my past experience and the low price.

As a general rule, I avoid buying stabilized businesses unless they provide extremely strong cash flow after the mortgage/ debt payments. When calculating my expected returns from a business or real estate investment, I never factor in appreciation—that is simply icing on the cake. I only factor in cash flow and the value created from bringing something from a low operating level to a stabilized level. Don't fall for the greater fool theory—i.e., I was a fool for buying a business or asset that didn't have cash flow, but there will be a greater fool that comes around and will buy it from me for a higher price.

Keep buying and selling costs as low as possible.

The fees involved in any transaction can be significant, so you need to keep them as low as possible to maximize your returns. What is potentially the biggest transaction cost in any deal, whether it's a business or real estate? The broker's fee or commission. Avoid using brokers and go directly to the seller if at all possible. If you have to use a broker, make sure he/she is experienced and adds value to the transaction through his/her industry or local knowledge.

Problems become opportunities.

Learning to deal with nonstop issues and problems is a true entrepreneurial skill. You have to learn how to face them (don't, *don't* ignore them!) and get through them if you are going to obtain your goal of financial freedom. Staying calm in the face of a storm is a key skill to learn. A lot of times you need to take a step back from the problem by consulting a mentor or group of peers and getting their feedback and experiences. In almost every case, someone else has faced and solved your problem! You also need to constantly watch for the next problem—changes in government regulations, changes in the economy, new competition, etc. The really good business owners anticipate problems before they happen, or in their earlier stages, when they are usually much easier to solve. I will tell you that the more experience you get, the easier the problems become to solve! You need to change your mind-set to view problems as opportunities!

M$M Star Tips

GET TESTED

Finding out your strengths and weaknesses at an early age is key to any future success. Places like Kolbe.com, strengthfinders.com, and myersbriggs.org are cost effective ways to get tested. Successful people focus on their strengths and compensate for their weaknesses by hiring the right people.

Know when to sell.

The old mantra, especially with real estate, is that you hold your investment forever and have the residents pay off your mortgage. I agree with this to an extent, but I am always willing to sell for the right price. I believe there will always be a "next" deal. For example, I sold all of my midsize apartments in Florida in 2006 for large profits. Every property I owned in Florida from 2003 to 2006 went into foreclosure within three years after we sold when the Florida real estate market crashed. Had I held on, I would've been struggling big time, especially if we'd needed to refinance. My rule of thumb in the mid-2000s was that if I could quadruple (i.e., a homerun) my investment within three years of purchase, I would sell. Because of the slower economy, I have backed the rule down to tripling my investment (I include cash flow into this calculation). Another example was my first deal selling the broker-dealer. The stock market was rocking in the late 1990s, and I had grown the broker-dealer hugely over a six-year period, but I really felt like it was time to sell as I could hit a "home run" (four times my initial investment) and the big guys were overpaying for the smaller firms. The sale proved to be timely, as we got fully paid out through the year 2000, and the market has been flat or negative since then.

Knowing when to sell also comes into play when you have to "cut your losses." This happened to me in both the lawn-cutting business and the franchise area developer business. I got out of both within five months after purchase as I realized I was never going to make money at either. Take your lumps, learn from them, and move on. Don't stay in a business that is not cash flow positive—it drains you financially and mentally. My two buddies stayed in the same franchise biz for a couple of years and ended up losing almost $500K, versus my $30K.

John Warrilow has written a good book called *Built To Sell*. In the book, he states that the most valuable businesses are the ones not overly dependent on the owner. He lists three criteria for saleable business:

1. The business must be teachable; you want a great set of employees (unfortunately, because of health costs and lack of work ethic, the smallest number possible) who know the business inside and out. Hire good employees and give them the incentive to stay.

2. The business must be valuable—i.e., a business that is not a commodity.

3. The business must be repeatable, with documented systems in place.

If you want to build future value, become an expert in these three criteria. The goal is to make the business independent of you as the owner. I have done this with my real estate business—I could be gone for a month and the profitability of the businesses wouldn't change. I heavily incentivize the managers (monthly bonuses based on profitability and occupancy) so the business becomes independent of me.

SECTION 5 § CHAPTER 4

YOU'RE GONNA NEED SOME COIN

One way or another, you're gonna need some coin to get started in any M$M venture. I know we all would like to believe that "no money down" deals are the norm in business and real estate, but they are one in a million. When you first start out, you will be scraping to come up with down payment money to buy a business (remember, M$Ms do not do start-ups, as they are speculative in nature and their failure rates are much higher than buying an existing business with a positive cash flow!).

Your number one source of funds should be your own savings. As I advise in "M$M Money Skillz," when you are under the age of thirty-five, put all of your extra income into a liquid account that you can use to invest in your business or real estate. Outside of your own money, here are the best places to get money when you are starting out:

Parents or friends—You need to be careful here, because when you mix business with family and friends, you can ruin relationships if things don't work out. You need to have three things in place before you go ask parents or friends for money:

   a. A well-thought-out business plan for buying a business that provides cash flow from "day one" (i.e., how you're gonna pay them back).

   b. Experience in that business or industry.

c. A letter for them to sign acknowledging that there is a lot of risk in any business and they could lose all their investment.

As long as everyone is on the same page and aware of the risks, parents and friends are your best sources of money. When I bought the broker-dealer back in 1997, I borrowed $200K from my dad and $200K from the bank.

Believe me, my dad made me pay off all the money with interest as soon as I could (within twenty-four months, I paid him back everything). In these situations, the loans strictly involve an interest rate and no equity positions.

A real estate agent we work with to find affordable residential rentals has the opposite story. He borrowed $500K from his mom and dad, who remortgaged their house after having it paid off, to invest in a health club (not a good idea). The situation worked great for a few years, but that business tanked along with the rest of the economy in 2008, and now he is struggling to pay them back. Not a fun situation to be in.

Partners—As with family and friends, partners are also usually people you know, with the difference being that these people are not as interested in receiving an interest rate for their money they provide; instead, they want an equity stake, i.e., they want part of the monthly profits or future sale profits of the business. Partners are very necessary in the beginning of any venture, but partners can be tricky. *Here's the number one rule with partners: always maintain 50.1% of the equity!* Equal partners rarely ever work out and often end up in a messy "divorce." You want "silent" partners who can provide advice when asked, but have no voting control in the business. You don't want your business idea hijacked by someone else just because he/she has money.

Here are a couple of tips for dealing with partners or investors in your business:

a. Detail your role (finding the deal, taking all the risk with the lender, and operating the business).

b. Get a good partnership agreement from your local attorney (use a smaller firm, as big firms way overcharge) that clearly states the risk, which includes loss of principal.

c. Offer them a rate of return that they can't get elsewhere. I pay 10%–12% annual distributions, which are sent monthly (I find investors love getting the monthly checks), with an upside whenever the business sells. I definitely undersell the upside. Each deal is different, but I never promise more than 2%–4% per year, which usually corresponds with the debt pay down of the loan. It's best to under promise and over deliver.

d. Send out quarterly financial statements with commentary on the key events of the quarter, and be accessible for questions about the statements or the quarter.

e. Treat investors as valued customers and always remember to put their needs ahead of yours.

M$M Star Tips

Pay What?

The true net cash flow will determine what you should pay for the business. My rule of thumb: *Never pay more than three times the net income for the value of a small business* (less than $10 million in revenue). Brokers will try to push you for four or five times, but don't do it. When you submit your offer, I would start at one or one-and-a-half times net income. One technique to use is to give the seller his or her price, assuming it's not more than three times the net income, but stretch the payments out over three to seven years and let the seller finance the deal.

A very common situation in business deals or smaller commercial real estate deals is where one partner does all the work and another partner (or partners) provides all the cash for the down payment. This partner doing all the work and not putting up any cash is often referred to as the "sweat equity" partner. This partner has to find the deal, negotiate the terms, secure the loan, get the deal closed, and then oversee the property manager after the purchase. A typical arrangement in this situation is the partner doing the work gets a 5%–20% equity stake, depending on the size of the deal—I have seen as high as 49%, which is too much—plus a monthly management fee of 3%–5% of the total rent collected to make sure the business or property runs smoothly. The partner(s) contributing the cash usually only want(s) a specific rate of return, i.e., 10%–15% cash on cash plus future upside in equity, and to stay out of the day-to-day management. The "sweat equity" guy needs to be able to put together a professional package to demonstrate his/her expertise to the investor(s) and have systems in place to pay out monthly checks and provide quarterly property updates.

Warning: if your partners are not friends or family members, you may start to cross into securities law issues. I would strongly recommend that you take Gene Trowbridge's class on real estate syndication prior to entering into a deal—trowbridgecurriculum. com.

401(k)/Roth IRA—If you have money put away in a 401(k), IRA, or a Roth IRA, you can use the funds to directly invest in a business (see guidantfinancial.com) in an entity called a Rollover as Business Start-up (ROBS) or in real estate by owning rental homes or even the equity in an apartment complex or mobile home park in a self-directed IRA. (Equity Trust—trustetc. com—is great for these types of transactions.)

Hard Money Lenders—These guys like real estate better, as they can take the underlying property as collateral for their loan. If the business you're buying has hard assets, such as real estate or equipment, hard money lenders may be willing to make you a loan.

Local Community Banks—Banks prefer making loans to people who don't need money, but if you have a good business plan, positive cash flow, or hard assets, you may get a loan. Look for a bank with an SBA (Small Business Administration) loan program, which significantly reduces the bank's risk. Look for SBA leaders in your community or state (search "SBA lender rankings in [your state]"). Once you establish a good track record of repaying loans, it will be easier to get another. A negative with all banks is that they will require you to sign a "personal guarantee," meaning your personal assets are at risk if you default.

Large Banks—I would never consider banking with one of the top fifteen banks in the country because the local people have no decision-making authority and they only want to lend to people who have lots of deposits to put in their banks. Don't waste your time.

Hedge Funds/Venture Capital—If you are looking for a larger amount of money ($1 million plus), you will want to consider getting a loan from a hedge fund/venture capital firm, as they have replaced banks as the leading lenders to fast-growing medium-sized businesses. The hedge fund/venture capital loans come with higher interest rates and more strings attached, but they are willingl enders. Make sure you understand the restrictions they will place on your operations before you sign any agreements. Venture capital firms are similar to hedge funds but primarily operate in the technology and biotech areas.

Credit Cards—The guy I sold a portion of my financial planning business to financed most of it with over $100,000 in credit cards. He worked his a** off to get them all paid off within one year. Using credit cards is a risky strategy, as the interest rates are high and can go higher if you are late (check out the fine print). I would only go here if you can't find coin elsewhere.

Real estate investors have a couple of other options:

1. **Insurance Companies**—Insurance companies love good cash flowing properties, and they will provide full twenty-year amortizations (i.e., you won't have to refinance every five to seven years), good rates, and nonrecourse loans (nonrecourse means no personal guarantees). They typically like loans for $2 million and above and will require 30% down. The broker will usually require a fee totaling 1% of the loan amount; the fee is paid at closing. A great contact to find these companies is Baxter Bode at the Interlachen Group (interlachen.net).

2. **Fannie Mae or Freddie Mac**—The government-backed loan providers Fannie Mae and Freddie Mac are hot right now, as they make up a significant majority of the financing done on apartment and retail deals. The rates are great, and they will provide twenty-five to thirty-year amortizations with ten-year balloons (i.e., you must refinance in ten years) along with nonrecourse. There are numerous commercial loan brokers that can provide access to Fannie and Freddie financing. Only use the ones that are very experienced with these types of loans, as the paperwork with them can be a bit overwhelming.

3. **CMBS Loans**—Commercial Mortgage Backed Securitized loans are loans done by the big Wall Street banks (Citi, Wells Fargo, J. P. Morgan, etc.) and are designed for the bigger players in the real estate biz. They will typically only deal with loans $5 million and greater, with $10 million–$25 million being the sweet spot. The rates are good, the loans are nonrecourse, and you can get twenty-five-year amortizations with ten-year balloons. However, the paperwork is horrendous and the fees are steep.

M$M Star Tips

Let the Seller Carry the Load

Regardless of how you scrape up your initial capital, you will be better off if you find a business or real estate deal where the seller "carries the load," i.e., finances most of the deal. Most sellers are going to want to have the buyer put some significant money down, but many will finance up to 80% of the purchase price and sometimes 90%. The key is to find a seller that is looking to retire or is burned out on the business. A business owner that is retiring often doesn't want to pay all the capital gains up front (even though he/she should, as the current 20% rate is bound to go up in the future) and is looking for a steady monthly payment in retirement. Seller-financed businesses don't normally require personal guarantees like banks do.

SECTION 5 § CHAPTER 5

WHO WANTS TO OPEN A BARBERSHOP?

One concept that is way oversold in America is the franchise. The standard franchise pitch is that in return for 4%–8% of your sales (not net income, sales), they will provide you with an established model and brand that you can replicate in the market you purchase. What franchises don't provide you is cash flow for the first twelve months and oftentimes much longer. *Main Street Millionaires* do not buy businesses that don't have a positive cash flow from day one, so buying a new franchise is not an option.

Maybe the franchise concept worked thirty years ago when there wasn't an enormous amount of competition, but today's franchises are not worth the money or headaches. Who makes the money on franchises? The franchisors and their salespeople, like Ray and Joan Kroc (the franchisors of McDonald's) who were two of the richest people in the country during their time. Or Dave Thomas, the franchisor of Wendy's. Or the couple that founded Curves. The upfront commission earned by the salespeople for selling a franchise is a minimum of 5% and usually closer to 10-15% of the amount you invest.

What franchises do well is prey on burned-out people in Corporate America and sell them an unrealistic dream. It's reached the point that when you post your resume on CareerBuilder or

Monster.com, you automatically start getting emails touting the benefits of owning a franchise. In the vast majority of franchise purchases, what you are trading is a dreadful corporate job for a job that will require you to work more hours, get paid less money, and risk a good portion of your retirement. Don't listen to the tall tales the franchise salespeople tell you. They make you sign your life away with a thick legal document, called a franchise circular, which has every one of their liabilities covered.

I know so many people, including myself, who were burned by franchises:

- I bought into the area developer's position for a "cool" haircut concept franchise in the early 2000s in Orlando. After watching the first store operate for two weeks, I realized that no store would come close to making a profit. I immediately demanded my money back. I ended up settling and losing $30K.

- Friends of mine who invested in this haircut concept ponied up for three stores (a big push for the franchise salespeople is to sell you a pack of three or six stores, because they make a bigger commission). After getting all three stores up and running and losing money at each one, they sold them for a fraction of the cost, just to get out and stop the bleeding. They lost more than $500K on this debacle!

- Other friends of mine signed up for three tanning salons in Orlando (I never understood why someone would want to go to a tanning salon in Florida). Within eighteen months, they gave away the two stores for $0 because both were losing money. Their total losses were just under $200K, but they got out of their personal guarantees for their leases.

- Another friend was the area developer for a sub chain. He told me that at least 75% of his sixty-plus stores at the time were either just breaking even or losing money. In my opinion, the only people who succeed with franchises are the ones with a lot of capital to begin with who have the ability to do multiple locations (ten plus) and the good luck to land in a highly marketable location. The failure rate for franchises that are marginally capitalized and can do only one to three locations is as high as it is for start-ups—90% are toast within five to seven years.

M$M Star Tips

Don't Be Afraid to Go Ugly, Early

The "hot" businesses right now all revolve around tech or the smartphone (i.e., creating apps). I think the vast majority of people aren't making money in these start-ups anymore. Most M$M businesses aren't pretty, but they make lots of money and their potential customer base continues to grow. I'm a prime example—a guy with a law degree making a lot of money in the mobile home park business. I wish I had "gone ugly" a lot sooner in my career.

What a *Main Street Millionaire* <u>will</u> consider buying are existing franchises that show positive cash flow (you need to *closely* verify the numbers) and are significantly discounted in price. This is a situation where you will find a lot of burned-out sellers who just want to get out, so you need to low ball them on a price. Be careful to avoid purchasing a franchise that is less than two years old and has big numbers—many franchises start out hot because they are a new concept, and then the competitors show up around year three and the numbers go down dramatically. I personally would never buy a restaurant of any type under any scenario (even if the seller gave it to me) nor a retail business (except a pawn shop, which is a quasi-retail business), so that rules out many franchises for me. If you do decide to look at picking up an existing franchise, your due diligence must be detailed and thorough so you know exactly what you're getting into.

SECTION 5 § CHAPTER 6

BUMBLE, STUMBLE, FUMBLE...WIN!

Here's another area where corporate America and entrepreneurship are more similar than ever—failure. It used to be that failure only happened to entrepreneurs because of the risk involved. Nowadays, it's just as easy to experience failure in corporate America by being laid off, passed over for a promotion, not getting raises, etc. Whether you own your own business or you take the corporate route, you will experience failure. How you deal with it is what needs to be learned.

Even though I have had a decent amount of success in my career (and hopefully will have much more), I have also stumbled badly at times because I didn't have a clue what I was doing. Let me go through the failures with you:

- I did graduate from law school, but barely. I finished at the top of the...bottom fifth of my class. By my last semester, I think I went to ten total classes out of 150 plus. I hated it. It was theoretical garbage. Why did I go to law school? Because I went to a liberal arts school and majored in political science (and partying) and had zero skills. *Lesson learned:* Your education has to provide you with skillz that can make you money. I also learned not to be afraid of the lawyers, because the vast majority are nerdy little bookworms who you wouldn't hire to cut your grass, yet they are supposed to be "esteemed." Whatever.

119

- Then I promptly flagged the bar exam twice. I barely studied each time because I didn't see any use in it, but my parents pushed me hard to do it. *Lesson learned:* You have to get tested for your passions and strengths at an early age and never be afraid to follow your heart, even when it means going against family and societal "expectations."

- After law school I landed a gig in a large bank's management training program. Again, in my parents' and peers' eyes, an "acceptable" thing to do. I hated it—the meetings to plan meetings, the brownnosing, the backstabbing, ugh!—and quit after eighteen months to join a local "financial planning firm." I quickly realized that the financial planning business was not about providing quality financial advice but selling products you barely understood to anyone you knew. Having no sales experience, I flamed out after nine months and headed back to Corporate America because I was broke. *Lesson learned:* Before attempting any entrepreneurial venture, you have to have a thorough understanding of its core operations by working in the business, or you will fail miserably.

I was embarrassed by my lack of success in law school and failing at the financial sales firm because I wasn't meeting the expectations that I perceived others had of me. Once I learned that I had to follow my own path and ignore what others said or thought about me, the successes started to come. Fear of disappointing and failing others close to you is one of the biggest impediments to creating wealth.

Even after I succeeded, I continued to learn:

1. In my second gig in corporate America at the broker-dealer, the CEO of the insurance company that owned us was a conservative lawyer who did not like me. He threatened to fire me a couple of times because I was too entrepreneurial.

The only reason he couldn't fire me is that my performance was too good. His response was to sell me the business. Thank you! *Lesson learned:* If you produce, you get paid and survive.

Corporate America and being an entrepreneur are no different any more—you have to produce to survive.

2. After we sold the broker-dealer to a large national insurance company, I quit within nine months even though I had a guaranteed three-year contract at $150K+ per year and a few phantom stock options. My boss was a corporate tool who made my life miserable because I was a threat to him. *Lesson learned:* Entrepreneurs don't belong in corporate America.

3. In the midst of selling the broker-dealer to the large insurance company, I went through a painful divorce that cost me a lot of heartache and over $500K after taxes. Nothing will make you feel more like a failure than divorce. *Lesson learned:* Don't get married until you are <u>at least</u> thirty years old.

4. After quitting the corporate gig, I promptly overpaid by about $400,000 for the financial planning business I bought. The sellers were using some questionable practices (such as selling customers 4% commission products and then charging them fees of 1.5% on top of that to "manage" the products). *Lesson learned:* Work your a** off to get out of a bad situation (which I did) and do more due diligence up front. Buyer beware.

5. In Florida, I lost $30K on a landscape company and $30K trying to be the area director for a "cool" haircut franchise concept. Stupid! *Lessons learned:* Never buy a business you have not worked in for at least two years and don't be afraid to cut your losses when you are in a non-cash-flowing business.

I have also stumbled in the apartment business:

- We were two weeks away from closing on the sale of our first turnaround property in Florida and I walked around a corner of the building and saw smoke billowing out of a unit, which delayed the sale. The problem was that I had already committed all of my capital to the next apartment deal (I had $2,000 left in my checking account) and needed a $900,000 short-term bridge loan to stay afloat until the first apartment deal closed. Talk about stress! *Lesson learned:* Never get overextended!

- When we bought our third property, I quickly realized the $100K in annual cash flow we were expecting didn't exist because the seller, a large REIT, deliberately showed us phony expense and bank statements (I now assume they had two sets of books and two bank accounts). We were very lucky to resell for a small profit nine months later as that property went into foreclosure two years later. *Lesson learned:* Be leery of the big corporate players in any business, as they are ruthless and consider lawsuits as a "cost of doing business."

- I almost lost $400K when I decided to do an option to purchase on a mobile home community from a guy I trusted (he had sold me a previous property which worked out well for us). Turns out he was tangled up in a massive Ponzi scheme. I was fortunate to buy that same property out of foreclosure after the Ponzi scheme imploded and made my money back, plus a bunch more. *Lesson learned:* Be very, very careful who you trust in business, as "greed" will do strange things to people. Never, ever give up.

I have also stumbled in the tax game:

Another failure I had related to taxes. I had two equal partners (never again) when I bought an independent financial planning broker-dealer from a local insurance company in Wisconsin. My role as president of the firm was the hard-charging sales guy who brought on more financial planners. I had very little clue about cash flow, accounting, or taxes. I left that up to one of the other partners, who was the "operations guy," and his buddy, who was our certified public accountant.

As you may recall, the stock market was booming back then, and we got a terrific offer to sell the firm to a larger national insurance company in the spring of 1998. We had bought the business for approximately $1.2 million ($400,000 each) and sold it for approximately $9.3 million, a phenomenal gross return of $2.7 million apiece above our initial investment. Even more phenomenal, we sold it nine months after we bought it.

The problem was, based on the advice of the "operations guy," who supposedly had consulted with the CPA, we did the sale on an installment-sale basis. The "operations guy" had told us the first payment, which was the smallest of the four, would be taxed at short-term capital gains rates (considered ordinary income and taxed at about 45% in Wisconsin at the time) and the remaining three payments would be taxed at long-term gain rates, which were about 22% (federal and state) at the time. When the time came to pay the taxes in year two of the installment sale, the CPA gave us a tax bill and it was double the amount we expected— it was all taxed as short-term gains. I immediately called the "operations guy" and asked for an explanation. He blamed the CPA, the CPA blamed him, and round and round. The ugly result: we all had to pay short-term gains rates on all payments— an additional $462,000 in taxes each! If we had just waited an additional three months to sell the firm, we would have saved $462,000 each! Ouch! After that episode, I made it a priority to learn the tax code. I got into the multifamily apartment business in the early 2000s in Florida and was able to sell a sixty-four-unit building for significantly more than I paid for it a short time later. This time, I waited more than eighteen months (just to be careful) to do the sale, I didn't have any partners, and I definitely made sure I paid long-term gains rates. It is worth your time and effort to learn as much as you can about taxes.

I have also failures and setbacks in my personal life:
My divorce was a brutal experience and, in my mind, a complete failure on my part. A sad side effect of my divorce is that it caused a huge rift between my mom and me (it's a long story). She died somewhat suddenly of cancer in 2007, and we never fully reconciled.

Another setback I had involved a good friend of mine named Mark McKenzie. Mark was involved in an unfortunate shooting accident with one of his other friends at the age of fourteen and became a quadriplegic. I got to know Mark well in high school and became close friends with him. We hauled him to all the parties, football games, dances, etc., through the years. When I got married the first time, I asked Mark to be in my wedding. He was excited and told everyone he was "sitting down" (instead of standing up) in my wedding. At the reception, Mark was the star of the party as he led the conga line around the dance floor in his wheel chair. Unfortunately, Mark died that night in his sleep. I still think of him often, as the thought of what a great guy he was with all the difficulties he faced still gives me a ton of inspiration.

An interesting stat is that most millionaires fail fourteen times before they make their first million. I am getting close. Failure is not easy when you are going through it, whether you are Steve Jobs getting fired from Apple in the 1980s or a small business owner who lost a business. But you realize as time goes by that failure is only temporary and you have to develop a faith in yourself (or a higher power) that will allow you to keep moving forward. Trust me, even though it's a cliché, you will learn way more from your failures than your successes. I truly believe that I never would have become an M$M if I hadn't failed so many times. I heard a phrase recently that made a lot of sense: if you truly want to achieve financial freedom, you have to commit to your own *Declaration of Independence from Corporate America* and see it through, no matter how many times you fail.

SECTION 5 § CHAPTER 7

GETTING A BIG CHUNK OF CHANGE...PRICELESS!

One of the things I didn't appreciate enough when I was younger was the gift of a big chunk of change when you sell a cash flow asset. I assumed everyone had these opportunities, but as I got older, I realized how rare they really are. The vast majority of people work in Corporate America, and their expenses are in correlation to their net paycheck. They never get the opportunity to get a large check—i.e., a minimum of $250,000 after taxes. A small percentage of corporate workers are lucky enough to get decent bonuses—$20,000 to $100,000—every couple of years, but after 40% is sliced off for all the taxes owed, the amount left over is usually quickly spent on a vacation, home improvement, etc. This is a nice scenario, but not close to the priceless scenario.

Getting $250K or more net at one time is huge because it catapults you toward M$M status at a much faster rate than otherwise possible. Unless you become a Fortune 500 CEO or CFO, the only way you can get a big chunk of change is by *owning an asset* (i.e., preferably a cash flowing business or a nice commercial real estate property). You need to buy it right, work hard to improve it, and then sell it for a big chunk of change after a few years or many years. You will never get a chance to get a big chunk of change by being in middle management in Corporate America.

PLEASE USE PROTECTION

In order to get a big chunk of change, it's important to keep your assets protected. There are many pitfalls in business and real estate, especially considering our "sue-happy" culture, so it's important to protect yourself. Here's what you need to do:

a). **Put all of your businesses or properties in a limited liability company (LLC).** We use a separate LLC for each property, and I would recommend a separate LLC for each commercial property you have. If you have only fifteen rental homes, I would just use one LLC. Remember, each LLC will require a separate tax return and separate annual records. (In North Carolina, they charge $200 per year for each LLC.)

b). **Get as much insurance as you can.** Insurance will be your best line of defense in almost any situation. We get $2 million of liability coverage on each property and we buy an additional $2 million in umbrella coverage. The umbrella coverage is cheap, so get as much as you can. One key to insurance is to find a good commercial broker that has a lot of experience in the particular real estate niche, i.e., mobile home parks or retail.

c). **Stay involved with the businesses.** If you tackle small issues before they have an opportunity to fester into bigger issues, you will save yourself a lot of money

KEEP IT IN THE FAMILY...

One of the coolest things about owning your own business, besides getting a big chunk of change, is that you can keep it in the family and pass it down over generations. I can't think of a greater gift you could give your children than a profitable business. We all know the job market is going to be brutal in the coming decade, so having a place where your children can work if they wish will become even more valuable in the future. I have seen several examples of people who have made a family business their priority, but two stand out:

- My college roommate Mike Vennetti's dad, Ralph, Sr., was a great guy (he passed away a couple years ago). He flunked out of three colleges without ever making it through a full semester at any of them. But he was a great salesman and he got a job selling heat transfer labels, which are the labels that are applied to the outside of detergent boxes, cereal boxes, etc. He excelled as a sales guy and accumulated some cash, so he decided to bet the farm and buy his own label business (two great M$M principles—work in the business first and buy a "go ugly, early" business). Within ten years the business became very successful. However, as his boys started to graduate from college, he decided to buy another business so all the boys could stay in the Chicago area and work for the business. So he leveraged to the hilt again and bought a liquid fill manufacturing business (it fills shampoo bottles for hotels, etc.) that became very successful. More important, it allowed his sons to work in the business and to stay together.

- The UPS Store by my house is owned by a man named Natu Prajapapi. He is an Indian immigrant who is a true entrepreneur inside and out. He has owned the local UPS Store for fifteen years, and it has provided him and his family a nice living. He lives modestly but has attained his version of financial freedom. Two of his nephews wanted to come to North Carolina from India, so he researched small businesses and discovered that convenience stores (another "Go Ugly, Early" biz) that were bought cheaply and improved could be very lucrative. So he put up $125,000 of his own money and borrowed $125,000 from a local bank with a personal guarantee. He bought one store for each nephew. The deal he struck with his nephews is that they needed to bust ass (they're in their early twenties) for the first five years before they could think about hiring a full-time manager and expanding into a second site. They also had to pay him back with a modest return, but they would own the business outright over ten years. Both young men have been at it for over three years now and have far exceeded all of their financial projections. They are well on their way to being M$Ms. What a great gift from their uncle!

Buying a business that generates cash flow has so many positives—the ability to obtain financial freedom, the ability to get a huge chunk of change when you sell, the ability to never retire if you wish, and the ability to keep it in the family. Sure, there are going to be a lot of headaches, problems, challenges, etc. (remember that *Main Street Millionaires* call these "opportunities"), but I believe the potential reward justifies the headaches. Go back to the question I asked at the beginning of this chapter: is there really more risk these days in owning your own cash flowing business or real estate versus staying in corporate America? I say a resounding *n-o-o!*

M$M Star Tips

An Apple a Day Saves Bucks

One big negative in owning a business is that health insurance is expensive. The cost for us to insure (health and dental) a family of four is in excess of $16,000 per year with a $5K deductible. If you have a serious illness, your cost will easily be double this if you can get coverage at all! You owe it to yourself, your family, and your M$M business to learn as much about wellness as possible and then practice it. Reduce stress. No smoking. No excessive drinking. Very limited fast food. Lots of fruits and vegetables. Lots of exercise. It's not easy, but you've got to do it.

M$M Star Tips

Don't Be Afraid to Give It Back

One of the key components of being an **M$M** is to be humble about the coin and be a good steward of your money. Whether you feel a compulsion to do it for religious reasons or for "karma" reasons, I strongly recommend you give away a minimum of 5% of your net income each year (working up to 10% over time) to people who are in need. My favorite charities are Raleigh Rescue Mission and Catholic Charities Food Pantry. If you are ever having abad day, go over to one of these places and get a dose of the reality that many people struggle through. Every time over the last twenty years that I felt like I was in a difficult position, I would go visit one of the charities and leave them a check for $5,000 or $10,000. As I would leave, I would be embarrassed for thinking my problems were even remotely close to those who don't have a roof over their head or food to eat. As we careen towards the point where 10% of the country owns 90% of the wealth, those of us in the 10% need to be as generous as possible in helping the less advantaged with our time, money, and talents.

A great example of giving back is Harris Rosen, who is Mr. Hotel in Orlando (he owns seven high-end hotels with little debt on them). He has given over $7 million to a low-income housing complex called Tangelo Park in Orlando. The twin focus of his program is to provide free day care to two- to four-year-olds and provide a free college education for all high school graduates of the complex. As a result of his gifts and focus on this complex, crime there has dropped 67% and the dropout rate has dropped from 25% to 6%! Awesome!

M$M BIZ SKILLZ RECAP

- Corporate America is a huge buzz kill. Entrepreneurship is the future.

- *Main Street Millionaires* only buy businesses that show a positive cash flow in the first month they own them.

- Work in a business before you buy it. Then you know the ins and outs.

- Scraping for coin to buy the business? Borrowing from family can be risky. Do it right or check out other options.

- Franchises are way oversold. New franchises are risky. M$Ms only buy businesses with positive cash flow. It's just not there with a new franchise.

- Don't make the new business about you. Build it as an asset or you'll never be able to sell it.

- Watch your backside. You've gotta protect your assets. Get insurance and understand taxes.

- Keep it in the family: what greater gift can you give your kids than a cash flowing business.

SECTION 6

M$M REAL ESTATE SKILLZ

100% of the shots you don't take won't go in.
~ Wayne Gretzky

There is no question that more millionaires have been made across the globe through real estate than any other avenue. Take a look at some of the names from the Forbes 400:

- **Donald Trump**—Where do you think Donald Trump got his start in the real estate business? From his dad, who was one of the largest owners of multifamily real estate in Brooklyn and Queens.

- **Richard LeFrak**—Often seen on CNBC, his family started in the real estate business in New York in 1901, primarily with multifamily. The third generation, led by Richard, has expanded from multifamily into office, retail, and other developments.

- **Sam Zell**—Also featured on CNBC a lot, this real estate entrepreneur started buying multifamily property around the University of Michigan during the mid-1960s when he was attending law school. He has gone on to form three of the largest REITs (real estate investment trusts) in the country—Equity Office Properties, Equity Residential (apartments), and Equity Lifestyle (recreational-vehicle parks and mobile home communities).

- **Jorge Perez**—Co-owner of the Related Group, he made his first fortune building and owning affordable multi-family housing in Florida in the 1970s and 1980s. He later became the condo king of Miami, which hasn't worked out that well for him, but he is still on the Forbes 400 list.

But the beauty of real estate is that you don't need to be a big guy to make a lot of money. It can be as simple as buying a few houses. In the late 1990's I owned a successful financial planning firm. If you remember that time, the stock market was in a big boom phase and everyone was scrambling to invest as much as they could in it. I had over $100 million in investable assets under management and nearly 400 clients. However, the client that I remember most was one of my smallest clients. He worked at the local paper mill and never made more than $50,000 in any one year. He had a small IRA with me, but I knew he had more money to invest because he was a saver, pretty frugal, and hardworking. I had a couple meetings with him, but couldn't convince him to invest more in the stock market. I asked him what he was doing with his extra money. He told me he was 50 years old and in the 10th year of his 15-year plan. His plan was buying an older, single-family house each year for around $50,000. He bought each house at a 15-20% discount from the market value because it needed work, which he was able to do himself and with a little help from some of his friends. He said he could rent it for $500/month, which was a little below the market rent, and keep it rented because "in good times or bad times, there is always a need for affordable housing in this country." His plan also included using all of his profits to pay off his mortgage as soon as possible. Being young and naïve at the time, I thought he was crazy to invest in boring affordable housing because the stock market was averaging over 20% returns each year.

I didn't see that client again for five years. During that five-year period, the stock market lost nearly 40% of its value, with those invested in technology stocks losing much more. When I saw him, I asked the client how life was treating him. He said he had just put in his retirement papers at the mill because he now had 12 of the houses paid off and his net income, after all expenses were paid, was over $60,000/year, more than he ever made at the mill.

More important, his net worth was now over $1 million. After hearing this, I thought to myself – why would you ever invest in the stock market when you could invest in affordable housing?

I have increased my net worth dramatically with my success in both the apartment business and the mobile home community business over the last ten years. I believe buying and owning affordable rental housing is one of the best long-term, wealth-building vehicles available today.

SECTION 6 § CHAPTER 1

CASH FLOW IS KING

I was always intrigued by real estate, but I had no idea how to get into the business. The one book that really inspired me was *Rich Dad, Poor Dad*, by Robert Kiyosaki. The book explained two of the coolest concepts ever— passive income and depreciation. The concept of buying commercial real estate and getting passive income (see below) with lots of tax benefits seemed like the ticket to me to truly becoming an M$M, especially after I had just finished paying a ton of taxes with the sale of the broker-dealer. But, again, I had no idea where to start, and, as I found out, the book made it seem a lot easier than it was.

Shortly after reading the book, I made my first foray into real estate investing when one of my financial planning clients referred me to a guy who was raising money for a condo development in Scottsdale, Arizona. He gave me the pitch about the great upside for the project and that I should conservatively double my $75,000 in a few years. Three years later, after receiving no interest or dividend payments, I was lucky to get my principal back.

My second foray into real estate almost ended in disaster. I saw an ad in the *Wall Street Journal* for an investment in senior apartments that guaranteed 15% annual returns. I talked to the developer on the phone and he seemed pretty straightforward, so I went down to Orlando and looked at a couple of his properties, and they seemed legit. I seriously considered sending him $100,000 in available capital, but something inside of me told me to hold off. It turns out it was a Ponzi scheme. All the investors lost their money, and he went to the pokey. Whew—dodged a bullet there.

After these two incidents, I realized I needed to take control of my own real estate destiny and really learn the fundamentals of the business. Below are the C-A-S-H-F-L-O-W fundamentals for real estate investing:

C – Cash flow properties only. Just like with businesses, I only buy real estate investments that show a positive cash flow in the first month I own them. Buying anything that doesn't have positive cash flow in month one is called speculation. *Main Street Millionaires* don't speculate.

A – Always buy from a motivated seller. Finding sellers who are motivated to sell, whether for financial reasons (such as divorce), medical issues, or management burnout, is key. It may take thirty low ball offers to find one motivated seller, but the effort is worth the reward. Having your financing lined up ahead of time for a quick close will get any seller motivated.

S – Start small. I started my real estate journey with a small eight-family in Neenah, Wisconsin. I now have over 3,000 units. By starting small, I got to see whether I liked the business, and if I made a mistake, it was going to be a small one.

H – Hire good managers. The best move I ever made in real estate was hiring a junior partner, Chris Barry, to oversee the day-to-day activities of the properties and to supervise the managers and maintenance personnel. Chris is great at these areas, and it's definitely not my strong suit.

F – Fall in love with the numbers, not the property. Nice-looking properties are great for showing your friends or relatives, but if they don't have positive cash flow, forget them. The number one criteria for purchasing a property should be its current cash flow and the ability to increase that cash flow.

L – Local yokels win out. Local knowledge is huge in real estate, as every market is different. I've drawn a circle that incorporates all the major metro areas (250,000 plus) within four hours of my house. I happen to have eight major metro areas within four hours of my house—plenty of places to invest that I can get to easily.

O – Own a majority of the property. I always own a majority of the interest in the LLC that owns each property, because it allows me to make final decisions quickly. One of the properties we manage, but don't have ownership in, has forty investors involved, with no one owning a majority. It's much harder to get things done with this arrangement.

W – Work the property yourself. There is no better way to understand the real estate business than getting behind the desk and dealing with tenants and maintenance personnel. I did it for several years as I got started.

Two fundamentals I love about real estate are the tax breaks provided by depreciation and the ability to enhance your returns with leverage. The tax breaks provided by depreciation are exceptional and allow you to shelter a lot of your current income from taxes, though you will pay it back when you sell a property. You can use leverage to significantly enhance your returns. A simple example: if you buy a property for $100 and pay all cash for it and net out $10 in profits, you are getting a 10% return on your money (10 divided by 100). If you buy that same property for $100 but put down 30% ($30) instead of paying all cash and use a mortgage from the bank to finance the other $70, your net will go down to $6 because you now have mortgage costs to pay.

However, your cash-on-cash return goes up to 20% (6 divided by 30). If you are operating in the millions, the numbers really add up.

The greatest gift that cash-flow-producing real estate investments can provide you is passive income, i.e., making money while you sleep. Earned income, which is what everyone gets in corporate America, involves exchanging your time and efforts for money. If you don't work, you don't get paid. Passive income is income received from an investment (bond, real estate, business, etc.) where the owner does not have to be directly involved in running the business. With real estate investments, once you get to a big enough level that you can hire a manager to run your property, you can significantly reduce your time involved with the property. For instance, I usually only go to my properties once per quarter. Passive income equals freedom!

SECTION 6 § CHAPTER 2

EVERYBODY NEEDS A PLACE TO LIVE

There are many different types of real estate to invest in. The most common are office properties, retail strip centers, warehouses, industrial properties, senior housing, student housing, self-storage, single-family residential, and multifamily. Within each area are niches. For example, in the office category one could specialize in high rises, suburban office buildings, or medical office buildings, to name a few. In the multifamily sector, it could be class A apartments (the nicest and most expensive) all the way down to mobile home communities. I have chosen to invest in affordable housing, whether it be single family rentals (SFR's), medium-sized apartment complexes or mobile home communities, for two primary reasons: First, affordable housing is a necessity. Everyone needs an affordable, clean, and safe place to live. And, second, the number of working poor is skyrocketing, so demand is booming for affordable housing.

Remember what my financial planning client said, that affordable housing does well in "good and bad times." Since the economic meltdown of 2008-2009, the demand for affordable housing has gone through the roof as millions of people have been forced to downsize. At the same time, the supply of affordable housing is at an all-time low as there has been very little affordable housing built in this country over the last 20 years – because the land and infrastructure costs are too expensive. This is an Economics 101 perfect storm: big demand with limited supply means prices are going up and occupancy levels are at all time highs, whether it be in affordable single-family houses, affordable apartment complexes, or manufactured home communities. And I don't see any let up in this scenario as more and more middle class Americans fall into the lower class due to lower paying jobs and higher costs for everyday necessities like gas, groceries, education, health care, etc. Fortunately for my business, and unfortunately for the country (in my opinion), the gap between the rich and the poor continues to grow wider, which increases the demand for affordable housing. More than 50% of the country now live in a household that makes less than $44,000/year, which means they can only afford $500-$700/month in total housing expenses. Recent statistics show that nine out of the ten most prevalent jobs needed in this country over the next 5-10 years will pay between $8-$12/hr. As one of my friends in the industry, who used to be a Wall Street guy and quit to own affordable properties full-time, said recently, "I love waking up every day knowing the demand for my product is only getting stronger."

The greatest thing about investing in affordable housing is that you can be part of the solution as well. We provide our residents with safe, affordable housing in clean and well-kept communities. We make a strong effort to get residents involved with each other by sponsoring activities on all the major holidays, putting in new playgrounds and soccer fields, planting a community garden, and coordinating with local organizations, such as the Boys & Girls Clubs and local food trucks, to provide services to our community. The biggest mistake you can make with affordable housing is not reinvesting in the complex or community. Re-paving the parking lots and/or community streets or rehabbing older apartments and/or homes every few years is a must. Slum lords are driven out of business quickly. Owners who treat their residents with respect (our policy is "firm, but fair") and reinvest in their complexes or communities will be the ones that thrive.

However, you need to understand one point clearly—you cannot be a "slumlord" and succeed anymore. You need to have safe, clean properties that are staffed with great employees and provide excellent customer service. I always try to have the "best product at the best price."

MY APARTMENT COMPLEX JOURNEY

I decided that if I was going to be in the real estate business, I had better have control of the process. About a year prior to reading Kiyosaki's book, I had hired on a junior partner at my financial planning practice who was right out of college, Chris Barry (his dad was a client of mine), and he was interested in the real estate concept as well. We formed a deal in early 2002 where I would put up all the money and he would manage the property. I got 80% of the profits, he got 20%. So we bought a little eight-family apartment complex in Neenah, Wisconsin—good old Stanley Court—for $300,000. The one thing I discovered is that the banks liked financing the apartment buildings if you had 20% down (I had no clue about seller financing back then). We made about $500 per month profit on this gem, and the tax loss helped me (because of the depreciation), so we decided to keep doing the business.

We bought a little four-family ($160,000) and then a twenty-four unit ($1,200,000), both in Appleton, Wisconsin, within the next couple of months. I loved finding and doing the deals, and Chris loved being outside and managing the properties. We weren't making great cash flow but earned close to a 10% cash-on-cash return on our investment plus the debt pay down. When we were closing on the twenty-four-unit building in early 2002, I asked the seller why she was selling. She told me she was liquidating everything in Wisconsin and reinvesting in Florida. I thought it was a gutsy move and I was intrigued by it. So I started doing research.

I had been to Florida on vacation several times, but I had never considered moving there. All the articles I read said that Florida was just about to boom, so I started looking for apartment buildings for sale on this new website called loopnet.com and in ads in the *Wall Street Journal*. By this time I had figured out how to analyze the apartment investments on a one-page Excel spreadsheet (I still use it today). The numbers I was seeing in Florida had far greater cash flow than in Wisconsin, primarily due to lower expenses (especially taxes and winter-related issues) and increasing rents.

I gave Chris a great Christmas present in 2002 by telling him I was going to liquidate everything—my new house I had owned for less than eighteen months, all my mutual fund and annuity investments, the financial planning business, and the apartments we had just bought—and move my family to Florida to invest in apartments. He thought I was out of my mind, but even though he was getting married that following summer, he agreed to go with me. So in a furious four months, with Chris's help, I liquidated everything.

Luckily, we broke even on the apartments (sold two for small profits and got beat up on the four-family); I sold the financial planning practice for a small profit, sold my house (got spanked on that by about $20K), and liquidated all of my investments. I had some coin, but no job, no house, and just nine months of limited experience in the apartment business.

I can't tell you what it was, but I had this strong instinct inside of me telling me to go for it. I was taking the biggest risk of my life at age thirty-eight, but I just went for it. All of our friends (I had gotten remarried) thought we were nuts. I think my wife, Becky, thought I was a little nuts as well, but she believed in me and went along for the ride. And what a ride it has turned out to be. We spent just under four years in Orlando, where Chris and I did a ton in the real estate biz.

1. We bought and sold seven midsize (64 to 120-unit) apartment complexes that increased my net worth by $1.5 million!

2. We bought and sold our first mobile home park (eighty-four units on less than four acres—a real gem). We only

owned it for ten months because we were in the process of relocating once again, but we did make a profit of about $75K on it.

I decided to sell in Florida because I started to sense that the economy was weakening and I was getting concerned about the increasing insurance costs that resulted from the hurricanes of 2004 and 2005. However, I owe a great deal to my commercial real estate broker and buddy Enon Winkler, who brought me great buyers for a couple of my bigger properties when I didn't have them listed. The funny thing is that I was resistant at first to selling even though the offers from the buyers were for much more than I had paid because the properties were cash flowing so strongly. Enon convinced me that the real estate mantra of "there's always another deal" was true. He was right. One of the main reasons I have chosen to stay a medium-sized owner (instead of large syndicator) is that when I first started in the apartment business in Wisconsin, I met a successful investor named Cal Aiken who had over six thousand apartment units at the time. He had almost one hundred employees, including a bunch of regional managers. He told me if he had to do it all over again, he would keep it small (1,500-4,000 units) and enjoy his life more. He said that you have the potential to make more money as you get bigger, but you also get a lot more headaches. I have followed his advice and am very happy I did.

So how do you get started in affordable housing investments? Here are the six steps to follow:

1. **Get educated.** Any good business requires hard work and basic principles you need to understand so you don't make a big mistake on your first investment. You need to invest in education materials that provide a step-by-step process on how to invest in affordable housing.

2. **Find a mentor.** You need someone with experience in the business who can guide you through your first couple investments.

3. **Select a geographic area where you want to invest.** I like the Southeast and Midwest U.S. as they are more affordable.

4. **Choose your affordable housing investment type.** What do you feel more comfortable with – single family homes (the easiest to get started with), apartment complexes (the easiest to get financed), or mobile home communities (the easiest to manage)?

5. **Put together a team.** You will need to find good local brokers, a local banker to finance your properties, a good CPA to handle your taxes, and a good property manager to oversee them.

6. **Put together a plan.** You will need a 1-year, 3-year, and 5-year plan that includes how many units you will buy, how much money it will take to acquire the units, how you will manage the units, etc. I have always found that written, measureable goals provide great accountability and are a great help to reaching your goals.

SECTION 6 § CHAPTER 3

ROOKIE MISTAKES

When I moved to Florida, I was super excited to get involved in real estate investing on a full-time basis. The problem with being too excited was that I jumped at a deal that I didn't really understand. The first property I bought in Orlando was called Catalina Isle (we nicknamed it the Izzle for Shizzle). The property was a half-mile from a solid middle-class neighborhood. The problem was that the half-mile distance contained a major freeway. I bought on the wrong side of the freeway.

Mistake #1: I didn't understand the local real estate market. Once I bought the property, I quickly realized that the seller had put "lipstick" on the property and didn't do a true rehab. I was too cheap at the time to pay $2,500 for a professional inspection of all areas of the apartment, including the flat roofs (a big no-no in Florida). That $2,500 easily cost me $35,000 in repairs that I could've extracted from the seller.

Mistake #2: I didn't pay to get professional due diligence performed prior to closing on a deal. Amazingly, the property cash flowed every month and I sold it for a decent profit eighteen months later. The reason I was able to come out ahead was that I didn't make the other rookie mistakes that are very common for newbies in the real estate game.

Mistake #3: Not having a team in place. The first member of the team you need is a broker. In commercial real estate, having "connected" brokers is very important. I like analytical brokers versus pushy sales brokers. Chris Clay from CB Richard Ellis in Norfolk, Virginia is a prime example of this new breed of broker who really understands the numbers. Other key team members are a commercial mortgage broker or community banker (my banker John Hintze at First National Bank, Fox Valley in Oshkosh, Wisconsin is one of the best in the country), a commercial property inspector, a commercial appraiser (don't overlook building these relationships), and a good CPA who understands real estate accounting.

Mistake #4: Starting too big. I started with a small eight-unit property and bought two other smaller properties before I ventured into a ninety-unit deal. A lot of real estate investors start by buying one single-family residential house, rehabbing it, and then renting it out. Starting small allows you to make mistakes that don't cost you a lot of money.

Mistake #5: Not having ample cash reserves. Unforeseen expenses, especially with repairs or capital expenditures, will always pop up when dealing with real estate. I always pad my reserves by 10%-15% before I purchase any deal, just to be safe.

Mistake #6: Overpaying for a property. You want to avoid this mistake because you may never do another deal if you lose money on your first one. The biggest reasons for overpaying are not understanding the pricing in the local market and using the broker's *pro forma* numbers instead of a conservative version of the seller's actual numbers.

Mistake #7: Paralysis by analysis. I see a lot of real estate investors overanalyze every deal. They make a lot of offers, but never closeon a deal because they always find something wrong with the property. Every real estate deal has a little "hair of the dog," meaning no deal is perfect. You need to do proper due diligence, but you also have to take action and get the deal done!

M$M Star Tips

M$M Five Star Tip: Steve Davis
Will Get You Started

If you are a rookie and new to the real estate game, I would recommend that you join Steve Davis' coaching program (gettotalfreedom.com). He has taught thousands of investors over the last 20 years and he specializes in people new to the industry. He provides a great platform for people with full-time jobs to get an extra $1,500 - $5,000/mo. in passive income from real estate.

Cost is $17/month – super cheap!

SECTION 6 § CHAPTER 4

NEVER PAY MORE THAN A 10 CAP

The primary factor I look at when sorting the properties is cap rate. Because I am a cash flow investor, I will never buy a property with a cap rate less than 10, with one exception. I will buy below a 10 cap when I feel the property is significantly mismanaged and can be quickly (within 6 to 9 months) raised to a 10 cap with minimal effort. My goal is to buy a property with a current cap rate of 10 and increase the cap rate to 15–20 by adding more homes (for mobile home communities), increasing rents (apartments), trimming expenses, etc.

What is a cap rate? A cap rate is a mathematical formula that is derived by dividing the net operating income (NOI), which is the gross income minus all of the operating expenses (does not include the mortgage or depreciation costs) by the purchase price. For example, a property that is selling for $1,000,000 and has a net operating income of $100,000 is selling for a cap rate of 10.

$$\text{Cap Rate} = \frac{\text{Annual net operating income}}{\text{Selling price/cost}}$$

There are a bunch of tricks to learn with cap rates. The best advice I can give you is to read as many books as you can on real estate investing. I would also encourage you to listen to real estate webinars and go to real estate boot camps. The more education you have on a subject, the more prepared you will be to invest. If you are really serious about the business, I would encourage you to get your CCIM (Certified Commercial

Investor Member) designation. Finding a mentor in the business will really improve your learning curve as well.

I have to state it again: *fall in love with the numbers, not the property!* The property may have great amenities and look really cool, but if the numbers don't add up to solid cash flow from month one (a minimum cap rate of 10 and a minimum cash-on-cash rate of 15%, i.e., if you invest $100,000, you need to receive a minimum of $15,000 peryear in return to consider doing the deal) you need to pass. There are a lot of properties you are going to love at first sight, but keep the emotion out of it and rely on the numbers. When you fall in love with a property and overlook the numbers, you commit a fatal act in real estate—overpaying for a property. I have made this mistake at least three times, and I was fortunate to lose money on only one of the deals. Be cautious with your numbers and remember that you make your money at the purchase!

In 2014, the cap rates have gone down significantly (we're back to the 5-6 range for the nice commercial properties) as the Fed has driven the interest rates artificially low trying to entice investors into riskier assets. I have adjusted my strategy a little as I will go down to an 8 cap for a purchase, but I will only do this if I know I can get the property to a 12 cap within six to nine months with a few easy adjustments: raising rents to market, passing through utilities, or rehabbing and selling existing vacant homes on the property. Its easy to forget that interest rates can change quickly, especially if inflation hits. If interest rates go up, the value of the property has to go down. Remember, with commercial loans, you have balloon balances due five to ten years out. If you bought at a low cap rate because you got cheap financing and the rates go up dramatically, you are going to have a problem refinancing unless you are willing to kick in a significant chunk of money.

I like mobile home communities (see "M$M Real Estate Skillz #6") because you usually can find higher cap rate properties. The primary reason this is the case is that it's harder to get financing on the parks compared with apartments. The other reason is that mobile home park expenses typically average 35% of net income, versus 55% for an apartment complex, thus allowing for increased cash flow.

SECTION 6 § CHAPTER 5

DUDE, WHERE'S THE RENT?

Once you have purchased your property, the real work begins. Regardless of what anybody tells you, property management is not easy. I call property management the "nitty gritty" of real estate. Property management is all about managing the details effectively—collecting the rent (the most important), handing out delinquent notices, dealing with resident issues, etc. The biggest reason small real estate investors quit the business is they get burned out from managing their own properties. Residents can be a huge headache. What you will normally find is that 85% of your residents are great and 15% cause problems. When you have five-hundred-plus tenants, that 15% can eat you up. That's why good property management is vitally important and will determine the success or failure of your property.

Below are some tips on property management:

1. **Hire good managers and overpay them.** I learned this lesson the hard way, as we have gone through our share of property managers over the years. The managers at each of our properties have at least two years prior experience before joining us and have great personal skills.

2. **Have clearly defined systems and forms.** We have all the same forms and systems at each property. We use the *Rent Manager* software system for all of our properties. We use the same background check company (Internet based) at each company. We use the same bank to scan all of our money orders and use their online bill pay system. We have the same forms and operations manual for each property.

Uniformity is a must!

3. **Enforce the rules.** It amazes me the amount of properties I look at where the rules aren't enforced. The biggest lapse is in collecting rent. I see a lot of properties that have $10,000 to $50,000 in uncollected rents! I would never allow that. In our system, if you don't pay by the fifth of the month, we send you a ten-day notice to pay or leave. If you still haven't paid by the sixteenth, we go to the courthouse and file an eviction. And though we are empathetic with the struggles many people are going through today, owning a property is not a charity.

Finding honest and straightforward third-party management firms for commercial real estate can be quite difficult. Most third-party managers that I've encountered with multifamily properties nickel and dime you to death, which significantly lowers your returns. So I advise hiring one person to oversee your property managers. When you are starting out, that person needs to be you. When you get bigger in size (probably 250 units plus), you can hire someone. My junior partner, Chris, performs these tasks for us. He has become an expert in the property management business. We use the "good cop/bad cop" system at our properties. We portray the managers as the "good cops," as they deal with the residents most often, and we want the residents to feel comfortable in telling them what's going on at the property (residents love to gossip about other residents). The "bad cop" is Chris—he handles all of the serious delinquency issues and other more serious resident concerns. If Chris appears at your door, you know the situation has gotten serious.

Absentee property management and/or part-time management can quickly lead to disaster. Once a property goes bad, it is difficult to turn around. Going bad usually involves letting in people without criminal background checks or with weak credit scores. You need to stay actively involved in your properties and run them like a business. Technology will allow you to organize effectively, but there is nothing like being on-site. Being on-site will also allow you to nip issues in the bud before they become bigger.

One quick story on the joys of property management: We had two brothers in Orlando that did the maintenance at our properties. Their names were Charles and Chucky—go figure. Both were incredible workers, but neither lasted with us for more than eighteen months. We hired the first brother early on, but he started to lose his marbles…to actually go 'nutso'. I found him one day hiding in the maintenance shed; he felt people were spying on him and were ready to shoot him, neither of which was true. We ended up checking him into the mental hospital.

The second brother started with us not long after that. He was strong as an ox and barely said a word, but was a great worker. However, about twelve months into his job with us, we started to hear some complex gossip that he was "visiting" one of the female residents after hours, which we strictly prohibited. We confronted him on the issue and he 'fessed up,' but he also told us the bad news: he had gotten the resident pregnant and she was having triplets! That wouldn't have been quite so bad if he wasn't already married with two kids. We had no choice but to let him go.

Property management can be difficult, especially if you are doing it on a part-time basis, but if you can master the art, the long-term rewards of owning affordable rental properties are enormous.

SECTION 6 § CHAPTER 6

TRIPPIN' ON TRAILERS

I saw a recent headline in the *Orlando Sentinel* that made me chuckle: "Angry Landlord Crushes Mobile Home While Tenants Flee." This is the perception most people have about mobile home communities—that they are dirty trailer parks with very shady residents. I think that perception is way off base. The true M$Ms in the mobile home community (MHC) business operate clean parks that compare equally to a B-rated apartment complex. Most people snicker at Chris and me when we tell them we own MHCs. We laugh all the way to the bank. I think owning MHCs is one of the best businesses available that provides high current cash flow and long-term wealth building. Below are the reasons I like "trippin' on trailers":

1. **High barriers to entry:** They are not making mobile home communities anymore because of the high cost to develop them, and cities have moved away from wanting affordable housing. A lot of parks were "scrapped" and the land redeveloped over the last fifteen years .

2. **Incredible demand:** The demand for affordable housing started to reappear again in 2008, and it has exploded since. Between 2002 and '07 the industry lost a lot of good

residents, as they were able to obtain home mortgages even though they could barely pay their rent. Now those people are all back to renting, along with a slew of other formerly middle-class people who have been pushed onto the lower rung of society by the Great Recession. With the gap between the rich and the poor only growing wider over the next decade, the demand for affordable housing will only increase.

3. **Relative ease to manage:** We switched over from apartments to mobile home parks because they are easier to manage. Apartment properties require at least one full-time maintenance person, and the average resident turnover during a year is 50%. A mobile home park has significantly less turnover, as a majority of the residents own their homes and seldom move.

One of the sellers I bought a park from was named Bob Binns. Bob was an ordinary Joe who decided to take a huge risk back in the late 1970s and buy a mobile home community. This community had 175 spaces, and he gradually got it filled up with homes over a period of ten years. The park provided him a decent living and allowed him to send his kids to college. He and his family actually lived in the park (a triple-wide, no less) for twenty-eight years! He got the park paid off over twenty -five years and he netted a little over $3 million at the sale! A multimillionaire just from owning one community.

The family I sold one of my other North Carolina communities to has another great story. The father scraped together enough funds in his early thirties (the 1960s) to buy two one-hundred-unit parks in California and one in Washington State. He sold one of the California parks in the mid 2000's and cleared over $10 million after taxes! The other two parks are now paid off and provide the family with a *monthly* check of over $100,000! The sad thing is that he passed away less than two years after selling the park, and none of the kids work because they don't have to, which I don't agree with, but it's their life.

MY MHC JOURNEY

One of the last properties we decided to buy in Florida was an older eighty-space mobile home park in Lakeland, Florida. The eighty units were jammed in on less than four acres—you could almost stick your hand out a window and touch your neighbor's home. We only owned the property for nine months, but we did well with the cash flow and made money on it even though we only owned it for a short period. I sold because we were selling all of our apartments in Florida.

Once I decided to sell the apartments in Florida, I was forced to go outside of Florida to find deals because the prices were way too high in Florida and the cash flow deals were nonexistent. Chris and I looked at Georgia, Alabama, and Tennessee before settling on North Carolina. We've been in North Carolina for five years and have done the following:

1. Bought and sold two medium-sized mobile home parks that were cash cows but were located in too-small towns. Made a decent little profit on both.

2. Bought three decent-size communities (175-205 spaces) that were severely distressed, i.e., lots of empty spaces and poor performance. We rehabbed them over twenty-four to thirty-six months, which included adding over 150 new or repo mobile homes, repaving roads, adding landscaping, etc. This work greatly increased their value, and all three were cash flowing strongly. We pride ourselves on having some of the nicest communities in the state—these aren't your stereotypical "trailer parks." I decided to sell the communities in December 2011 because I got my price from the seller, and I knew that a slew of bank-owned deals that were going to hit the market between 2012 and 2014. The timing couldn't have worked better for me.

3. I reinvested the proceeds from my 2011 sale and have added a couple more investors to increase my holidngs to 32 parks with over 3,500 spaces. I was fortunate to find the distressed

deals like I thought and have found some unbelievable deals. I sold the parks at the end of 2011 for an average of $32,000/space and I bought the new communities for an average of $4,750/space!

Chris and I have created a nice business with the communities we own and the two that we manage. The business now generates over $10 million per year in rents with less than 20 employees! It's definitely not rocket science, nor the legal business. (Thank God!) Chris and I still chuckle—two college-educated grads becoming M$Ms by owning mobile home communities. Crazy. Do you think any high school or college guidance counselor in America is pushing any kids in this direction? I highly doubt it. *We* couldn't care less, as we know we are providing a great service to people (safe, clean, affordable housing) and it allows us to live the M$M lifestyle.

SECTION 6 § CHAPTER 7

STRENGTHEN THE CORE WITH A "SIX-PACK PLAN"

A new friend of mine, Craig Haskell, has done an excellent job of organizing a ton of practical real estate investment advice on his website, valuehoundacademy.com. I wish I'd had access to this information when I was starting out—it would have made my life so much easier. What I really like about Craig's philosophy is that he focuses investors on becoming "value hounds" in real estate, i.e., buying distressed property, rehabbing it, and then positioning it for a future sale or just reaping the cash flow rewards. As part of my in-depth study of Craig's material (I never stop learning) and because I am looking at so many deals now, I went back over my ten-plus years in the business and have solidified my core "six-pack" rules that I use for every deal. I find that if I follow my six-pack rules, I always make money.

The Six-Pack Rules

Only Buy Properties...

1. ...Within twenty minutes of a major metro area, which I consider having a population of 250,000 or more. Most large buyers of properties will only consider major metro areas for purchase.

2. ...That have significant upside in equity and cash flow. I like deals that are 60%–70% occupied that sell for prices reflecting this vacancy level.

3. ...That have positive cash flow from day one. I can never emphasize this enough.

4. ...Where the sales price is based on actual numbers, not *pro forma* numbers.

5. ...That are selling for at least a 10 cap on current numbers or a minimum of an 8 cap that can be quickly transformed into a 12 cap within six to nine months.

6. ...Focus your properties in one or two geographic areas as they are easier to manage and you can get economies of scale. The closer to your home the better.

If I follow these rules, I end up with properties that provide "the best product at the best price," and I know I will make money.

In my ten years of the business, there has never been a better time to be a real estate investor, as the deals are tremendous. I encourage you to follow the M$M skillz provided above and get educated in the real estate business. I am confident that you will have positive results.

One last story on real estate. A friend of mine named Doyle Slifer is a true real estate success story. Doyle had a tough upbringing (his dad committed suicide when Doyle was only five) that has led to an adventurous life, which has included getting his medical degree in Jamaica, of all places. Doyle dabbled in real estate through the years by owning a few houses, but he really liked the concept of the self-storage business. He decided to go all in and build a one-hundred-unit storage site from scratch in the central Illinois town where he resided. It took him a year or so to get it going, but he did so well with the first complex that he decided to buy some existing units and build another complex from scratch. Within three years, which included a year fighting cancer and doing chemo, he had eight hundred self-storage units. He now has over two thousand units and proudly states that he has made his children rich and has paid for all of his grandchildren's education with these units.

Guess at what age Doyle built his first one-hundred-unit self-storage facility? At the ripe young age of sixty-one! It's never too late to start! Doyle is now eighty-four, in good health, and he oversees the operations of all the units from his home in Florida because of the advances in technology. I asked Doyle when he was going to retire and, as a true M$M, he quickly answered "never!"

M$M REAL ESTATE SKILLZ RECAP

- More millionaires have been made across the globe through real estate than any other avenue.

- Affordable housing is in huge demand. Many folks can't afford to own or can't qualify for financing.

- Only buy properties that cash flow from day one. Appreciation is made at the purchase.

- Buy local. Managing anything more than four hours away is a challenge.

- Fall in love with the numbers, not the property.

- Avoid rookie mistakes, especially overpaying for a property and inadequate cash reserves.

- Property management is the nitty gritty of real estate. Hire good property managers and pay them well to manage the details.

SECTION 7

M$M ACTION PLAN

We know the financial situation in America is rapidly deteriorating for many people. The middle class is moving down to the working-poor category in ever-increasing numbers. The "American dream" is unfortunately not a possibility for a majority of Americans today, and I don't think things will get significantly better over the next decade as the huge amount of debt accumulated by both the government (federal, state, and local) and consumers is going to take at least a decade more to get under control, assuming it doesn't get way out of control.

We also know corporate America is a huge buzz kill and is now accessible only to the small percentage of Americans that have specific skills (A/F and STEM) and are willing to finance educations costing $100,000–$200,000. The legal and medical professions are not nearly as lucrative or enjoyable as they once were and now require huge education costs for limited job possibilities.

However, there are still possibilities to achieve financial freedom for those who are willing to break from the herd and go against the established "norms." First, you need to understand the M$M Money Skillz. The age of flash is over, as the financial pressures to live even a middle-class lifestyle are going to be severe as costs continue to go up, well-paying jobs become harder to get, and Social Security payments and Medicare coverage become a fraction of their current selves.

The "Three G" program (good grades, good college, good job) does not guarantee anything anymore. A vast majority of your education and skillz will be learned outside of the classroom, so you have to keep your education costs as low as possible. Zero student loans are the goal.

You have to take control of your own financial destiny, hopefully at the youngest age possible, and start owning cash flowing assets, like the M$M businesses and/or affordable housing properties. I do know that the good M$M businesses that provide quality and affordable services have great potential as the number of working poor explodes in this country as we, unfortunately, careen toward third-world status. Below is an action plan for the beginning M$M:

The M$M plan to skip college and get a huge head start:

Below is a simple plan that will greatly enhance your education and skills without setting foot on a college campus:

1. Live in your parents' basement (low or no rent), get an inexpensive car (no car payment), and keep your living expenses as low as possible.

2. Get tested—you need to hone in on your passions and strengths. Don't go into this blind. I recommend Strength Finders, Myers-Briggs, etc. (see "M$M Toolbox"). Cost: $50–$100.

3. Take at least one tax and one accounting class from H&R Block or the local community college. You need to understand the basics of cash flow accounting if you are ever going to own an M$M business or affordable housing property. Cost: $100 each.

4. Read as many personal finance, entrepreneurship, and real estate books as possible, including *Rich Dad, Poor Dad*, *The 4-Hour Work Week*, and others (see "M$M Toolbox").

Also, become a Google maniac and read as much content and participate in as many free webinars as possible in your area of interest. Cost at Amazon.com: less than $10 each.

5. Sign up for the online Dale Carnegie sales training courses (dalecarnegie.com). Every entrepreneur needs to know how to sell. I can't emphasize it enough. Cost: $299. Well worth it. Check out your local community college for its sales programs as well.

6. Join your local Toastmasters Club. These clubs help people practice their public speaking, which will be important in making sales pitches to clients or investors. Cost: $50.

7. Attend as many free classes on entrepreneurship and business skills as possible at the local community college's business department. Cost: $0.

8. Find a mentor in your specific field and ask him/her a thousand questions about how he/she did it. This is as important as learning how to sell. Don't be afraid to become a stalker. Most people love talking about themselves. Cost: $0, but it will save you thousands in mistakes.

9. Work in your field of interest for a minimum of twenty-four months before attempting any entrepreneurial venture. Cost: $0.

Below are M$M businesses you can get into without a college degree and hopefully own in the future:

Financial Services

Within the financial services industry, there are three primary areas where you can easily start on your path to becoming an M$M:

1. Pawn Shop—Every pawn shop is dying for good salespeople. Positions usually start at $10 per hour with commissions and bonuses. You can move up quickly here. The goal is to buy your own shop within two to five years. All you need to do is apply.

2. Insurance/Pension Sales—All this requires is an insurance license and getting hooked up with a local agency (they are always looking for good salespeople as well). I know lots of people making $250K plus in this business.

3. Tax Preparation—H&R Block and the other tax prep services can get you trained and get you started making money in the business. If you like the business and want to open your own shop, I would suggest getting your Enrolled Agent (EA) designation from the IRS (requires either a test or prior experience with the IRS). You will need to own multiple shops to make $100K plus, but the business is also seasonal, so you have lots of time off.

Real Estate Investing

Becoming a licensed agent/broker is a great way to get your feet wet in the business. You may not make much the first couple of years, but the experience will be invaluable. Focus on investors and learn to become a bird dog for them. The cost to get licensed: $500.

If you want to get further credentials in real es tate, I recommend the CCIM—Certified Commercial Investment Member (ccim. com)—program. It's a great program for those looking to branch out in commercial real estate. The program consists of several classes, tests, and prac tical experience. You can complete the program on a part-time basis over a couple of years at a cost of around $2,000. You can also learn a ton from the website valuehoundacademy.com. The founder, Craig Haskell, has done a great job of providing a dirt-cheap but incredibly accurate real estate education.

Fast Food

You learn a lot about business operations and customer service working in a fast-food place. Read Bernard Kelly's book *Flipping Burgers to Flipping Millions* and follow his path from working the fry machine to making serious coin with McDonald's by his early thirties. This career path is still readily available, though you may have to relocate to buy a franchise.

Retail

I am not a huge fan of retail, but I know store owners can make $100K plus, although it's a lot of work. Rent-A-Center and Dollar Store are always looking for good salespeople. The goal is to be managing a store within two to three years and then owning one within five to six years.

Drive Time and other auto dealerships are like retail in that they are dying for good salespeople. It's going to be a little easier to establish your own "buy here/pay here" shop, as you can start small.

I would add that all of these businesses, even if they are primarily brick and mortar, require strong Internet marketing skills. You are going to get a ton of leads from the Internet if you know how to position yourself properly.

You can definitely outsource this role, but I would take a class at the community college(a lot of them are free) or look at Tom Antion's training (greatinternetmarketing.com).

YOUR M$M ACTION PLAN

Take a few minutes to answer the questions below. This exercise will get you started thinking about your M$M Plan:

My M$M Education Plan
What are my strengths (from testing)?

What classes do I need to take at community college?

Where is the best place for sales training?

Where is my local Toastmasters club?

Websites/blogs/books I will follow and/or read:

M$M Business Preparation Plan

What businesses am I passionate about?

Where can I get a job in those businesses?

Who will be my mentor?

Where am I going to get money to begin?

What websites/blogs/books will I follow or read to learn about my business?

M$M REAL ESTATE INVESTMENT PLAN

Will I get my broker's license?

Will I enroll in the CCIM classes?Other websites/blogs I will follow:

Who will be my mentor?

Will I work as a property manager first?

SECTION 8

M$M TOOLBOX

TEEN'S TOOLBOX

Money Skillz:

- creativewealthint'l.com—summer money camps for teens
- chadfoster.com—teen's guide to personal finance
- *Ultimate Kid's Money Book*—Neale Godfrey
- Cashflow for Kids—board game for kids designed by Robert Kiyosaki (richdad.com)

Biz Skillz:

- nfte.com—youth entrepreneurship courses
- lead-America.org—summer entrepreneurship courses
- juniorbiz.com—follow the achievements of today's entrepreneur whiz kids
- successfoundation.org—go to the teens section for valuable resources and insight

YOUNG ADULT/COLLEGE STUDENT TOOLBOX

Money Skillz:

- getrichslowly.org—twenty-seven money tips for young adults/college kids

- *Debt Free U*—a book by Zac Bissonnette showing how to get the piece of paper for the least cost
- *The C Student's Guide to Success*—a book by Ron Bilwas

Biz Skillz:

- successmanifesto.com—Michael Simmons brings his entrepreneurship message to colleges
- sife.org—student entrepreneurship clubs with over eight hundred chapters at colleges across the country
- personalmba.com—Josh Kaufman teaches you what you learn in an MBA program for $30 instead of $50,000
- Real Estate Skillz:
- *Rich Dad/Poor Dad*—richdad.com
- *Real Estate Investing for Dummies*—Eric Tyson
- Testing Sites:
- kolbe.com
- strengthfinders.com
- myersbriggs.org

M$M JOBS TOOLBOX

Ten Most Profitable College Majors:

1. Engineering
2. Economics
3. Physics
4. Computer science
5. Statistics
6. Biochemistry
7. Mathematics
8. Construction management

9. Information systems

10. Geology (oil and natural gas fields)

Ten Lowest-Paying College Majors:
(You aren't doing these for the $$ but because you are passionate about them.)

1. Social work

2. Elementary education

3. Theology

4. Music

5. Liberal arts

6. Horticulture

7. Language arts

8. Hospitality and tourism

9. Philosophy

10. Drama

M$M MONEY SKILLZ TOOLBOX

Books:

- *Money Matters*—Dave Ramsey
- *Rich Dad's Conspiracy of the Rich*—Robert Kiyosaki
- *Living Large in Lean Times*—Clark Howard

Websites:

- cnbc.com
- cnnmoney.com
- msnmoney.com
- forbes.com
- everbank.com (gold, silver, metals info)

Getting Out of Debt:

- fieldofdebt.com
- couponing101.com

Highest Rated Insurance Companies:

- Allianz
- Jackson National
- Mass Mutual
- Met Life
- New York Life
- Northwestern Mutual Life
- Pacific Life
- Prudential

M$M BIZ SKILLZ TOOLBOX

Books:

- *The 4-Hour Work Week*—Tim Ferriss— fourhourworkweek.com
- *Crush It*—Gary Vaynerchuk—garyvaynerchuk.com
- *Get Rich Click*—Marc Ostrofsky—getrichclick.com
- *How to Buy a Good Business at a Great Price*—Richard Parker— diomo.com
- *The E-Myth*—Michael Gerber—e-myth.com

Magazines/Websites:

- *Bloomberg Businessweek*—bloomberg.com
- *Entrepreneur*—entrepreneur.com
- *Inc.*—inc.com

Businesses for Sale Listings:

- bizbuysell.com
- globalby.com
- M$M Real Estate Skillz Toolbox

Books:

- *Rich Dad Poor Dad*—richdad.com
- *Insiders Guide to Real Estate Investing*—Craig Haskell (valuehoundacademy.com)
- *Real Estate Investments & How to Make Them*—Milt Tanzer
- *The Millionaire Real Estate Investor*—Gary Kellor
- *Get Rich Slow* – John Webber

Other:

Asset Protection—Dyches Boddiford is the guru here—assets101.com

Raising Money—Gene Trowbridge has the best information— trowbridgecurriculum.com

Tax Rules:

- Diane Kennedy—taxloopholes.com; she was one of the original co-writers of *Rich Dad Poor Dad*
- *Every Landlord's Tax Deduction Guide*—a book by Stephen Fishman

Commercial Property for Sale Listing Sites:

- mobilehomeparkstore.com
- loopnet.com

Turnkey Real Estate Providers: (for single family home investing)

- buildrentals.com – Baltimore/Atlanta

- mackcompanies.us – Chicago
- memphisinvestmentproperties.net – Memphis
- realestatedone4u.com – Indianapolis

MORE ON THE M$M OPPORTUNITY

If you'd like to learn more, please check out my website and blog, or follow me on Twitter and Facebook for great ideas to get you on the path to becoming a *Main $treet Millionaire*.

Web and blog: www.mainstreetmillionaire.com

Twitter@MainStMillions

Facebook: Main Street Millionaire

Questions or ideas for things you'd like me to write about in my blog or next book? I'd love to hear from you. Send an email to the address below:

mconlon1@gmail.com